Shock

The Black Dog of Bungay

A Case Study in Local Folklore

by Dr David Waldron
&
Christopher Reeve

2010

About the Authors

Dr. David Waldron is a lecturer in history and anthropology at the University of Ballarat in Victoria Australia. His research interests include folklore, British history, and religious studies with a particular eye to the inter-relationship of history, social identity, religious belief and folklore. He has published numerous articles and collaborated in many publications on the development of folklore and religious beliefs from the English reformation to the present.

Christopher Reeve was born in Bungay, and educated at Bungay Grammar School and Norwich City College. He gained an M. Theol (Hons.) degree in theology and church history at St. Andrew's University, and a B.A. in Art History at the University of East Anglia.

He has published a number of local history titles including:

A Straunge & Terrible Wunder: the Story of the Black Dog of Bungay, 1988.
The Town Recorder: A History of Bungay in Photographs, (with Frank Honeywood), Vol. 1, 1994; Vol. 2, 2008.
Images of England: Bungay to Beccles (with Terry Reeve), Vol. 1, 1998; Vol. 2, 2004.
Paranormal Suffolk: True Ghost Stories, 2009.
Bungay: Through Time, 2009.

Acknowledgements

To the people of Bungay whose story has made this possible.

To the Bungay Museum

To David's father, Bruce Waldron, for his enormous efforts in assisting with editing and discussion.

To Norman Woods for his editing and commentary on local history.

To our families for all their support over the year.

To Tania for her gorgeous cover art.

To Clare Stubbs for her assistance in research and discussion.

To Martin Evans for assistance with the photographs.

This First Edition 2010

Published by Hidden Publishing

ISBN 978-0-9555237-7-9

www.hiddenpublishing.com   info@hiddenpublishing.com

Contents

Introduction 7

1. A Straunge and Terrible Wunder... 22

2. Life and Times in Elizabethan Bungay.. 47

3. The Black Dog of Bungay in Folklore.. 65

4. The Making of 'Old Bungay' 88

Conclusion 117

References 124

Appendix A.. 128

Appendix B 138

Appendix C.. 141

List of Illustrations 142

The Black Dog of Bungay painting by Tania Poole

Introduction

Finding the Black Dog of Bungay

The Church appeared a mass of flame

And while the storm did rage

A Black and Fearful Monster came

All eyes he did engage.

All down the church in midst of fire

The Hellish monster flew

And passing onwards to the quire

He many people slew.[1]

I would like to begin this book with a story of an encounter I had with a large dog during the process of writing. My family and I had visited a close friend's house and returned late in the evening about midnight. We busied ourselves putting the children to bed and I went out into the front yard of our home to feed our cat Treelo (named after a character in a children's television programme my daughter enjoyed) and bring him in for the night. Usually, I was unable to bring the cat in with a tap on his food tin, but not tonight, so I left him out and went to bed. Later that night we were awoken by a harsh screaming noise from a cat that sounded positively ghastly and rather unnerving at 2 a.m. I dressed myself and went outside into the cold foggy night thinking our cat was engaged in a fight with a stray. Strangely, while there was an awful caterwauling outside I couldn't at first see anything out of the ordinary. After a further investigation I found in the

1   Taken from the reprint of Abraham Fleming's 1577 pamphlet *A Straunge and Terrible Wunder* published by T & H Rood in 1826. Ethel Mann Collection: Lowestoft Records Office.

next-door neighbour's yard a large black dog with its jaws fastened over our cat, proceeding to slowly crush him while he screamed. I quickly ran over to the neighbour's yard and tried to distract the dog and possibly free our cat. While the dog was very solid and muscular, it was only slightly over knee high. But in those circumstances, at that time of night, it appeared to me to be impossibly huge with an enormously wide jaw. An immensely muscular crocodile was perhaps the best way I could describe the appearance of the dog with its wide shoulders and huge triangular head. I was not able to distract the dog's attention and returned home to grab the nearest item which came to sight, a bucket of water. By the time I had returned the dog had killed the cat with a rather sickening, audible crunch and turned its attention to me. I backed off slowly keeping my eye on the dog at all times with my bucket of water at the ready, feeling very conscious of wearing only a tracksuit and pitifully armed with nothing more than a bucket. The dog followed me closely with a constant low growl and leapt at me with a low bark and a snap or two of its jaws whenever my eyes wavered to see where I was going. I managed to find my way back to my yard and shut the gate. The dog left shortly thereafter. The following morning I went next door to bury our cat and break the news to the children, only to find that the dog had broken into the next-door neighbour's yard and was still there from the night before. It was quite amazing to see how a dog which had seemed to be such an enormous and vicious brute the night before, was now a perfectly normal, mid-sized dark brown Bull Terrier cross with a wagging tail and seemingly friendly demeanour.

I begin with this story, not because I wanted a simple rational explanation for the story of the Black Dog of Bungay, but because it illustrates something of the nature of humanity's relationship with dogs in general. The event on my front lawn led to a great deal of personal reflection on the nature of human experiences and how these are represented, the broader mythic and cultural associations that shape these representations and experiences, and their relationship to folklore. I remember at the time inexplicably having the thought pop into my head that this dog was a night-time predator that roamed the streets of my home town of Ballarat (a regional centre in central Victoria, Australia) and I had the misfortune to come across it when the daytime world was sleeping. If I was of a more superstitious mind I could have easily read a great deal into that night's adventures. For all that dogs serve as companions, guardians and guides they are also profoundly dangerous predators with a high degree of unpredictability. As the old saying goes 'There is a wolf inside every dog.' When coupled with the seeming sixth sense that dogs have, their use of superior hearing and smell and their fixation on death as carrion feeders, it is little wonder they have such a powerful role in most mythologies as guardians of the underworld, psychopomps, hell hounds and guides. In this sense, dogs are closely interwoven with human history, culture, folklore and mythology but there is a deep ambivalence in the kind of roles they play in these. It is in this context I want to look at the history of the mythology and folklore of the Black Dog of Bungay. In producing this book I have predominantly dealt with the post nineteenth century material in my own background as an anthropologist and historian, whereas Chris has contributed the chapters pertaining to 16th century Bungay and provided commentary and resources on much of the rest of the material in his capacity as the curator of the Bungay museum and author of numerous local history books, pamphlets and tracts.

Bungay

Bungay itself is a small country town of approximately 5000 people on the border of Norfolk and Suffolk, approximately 20 miles west from the coast. Located on high ground bordered by the River Waveney and located on the edge of the marshlands, it has been the site of numerous settlements and fortifications since the Neolithic period. A large fortified settlement was established during the Roman occupation until the fifth century; the Roman well still exists and was the source of the town's water until the 1930s. During the sixth century Bungay was settled by invading Saxon tribes. It is during this period that the town received its name 'Bunincga-haye' or 'Land of the clan of Bonna'. This period was marked by extensive settlement and the establishment of many burial-mounds still located on the town common. During the Norman period the town served as the seat of power of the rebellious Bigod family who built Bungay Castle, the ruins of which lie behind The Fleece Inn. Behind the medieval Church of St. Mary's lie the ruins of the Benedictine Priory established by Gundreda, widow of Roger Bigod, closed in 1538 under the dissolution of the monasteries. The centre of town is marked by the Buttercross where regular markets have been held since the middle ages. The 1688 Great Fire of Bungay still scars many of the town's buildings and walls with traces of blackened ash. Bungay is very much the epitome of the rural English town with a long history manifested throughout the landscape, architecture and local culture.

The town itself has a peculiar and gothic claim to fame. On August 4, 1577, during a thunderstorm of 'darkness, rain, hail, thunder and lightning as was never seen the like' it is claimed the Church of St. Mary's was attacked by the apparition of a huge spectral hound.

The 17th century Butter Cross in Bungay Market Place

Abraham Fleming, writing from London a month after the incident, vividly describes the events in the following tract,

> Immediately hereupon, there appeared in a most horrible similitude and likenesse to the congregation then and there present a dog as they might discerne it, of a black colour; at the site whereof, together with the fearful flashes of fire which were then seene, moved such admiration in the minds of the assemblie, that they thought doomesday was already come. This black dog, or the divile in such a likenesse (God hee who knoweth all worketh all) running all along down the body of the church with great swiftnesse and incredible haste, among the people, in a visible fourm and shape, passed betweene two persons, as they were kneeling upon their knees, and occupied in prayer as it seemed, wrung the necks of them bothe at one instant clefe backward, in so much that even at a moment where they kneeled, they strangely died... There was at ye same time another wonder wrought; for the same black dog, still continuing and remaining in one and the self same shape, passing by another man of the congregation in the church, gave him such a gripe on the back, that therewith all he was presently drawen togither and shrunk up, as it were a peece of lether scorched in a hot fire; or as the mouth of a purse or bag, drawen togither with string. The man albeit hee was in so strange a taking, dyed not, but as it is thought is yet alive: whiche thing is mervelous

in the eyes of men, and offereth much matter of amasing the minde...

Then, according to Fleming, the hound fled to Blythburgh Holy Trinity Church, the cathedral of the marshes where,

> ...placing himself uppon a maine balke or beam, whereon sometime ye Rood did stand, sodainly he gave a swinge downe through ye church, and there also, as before, slew two men and a lad, and burned the hand of another person that was there among the rest of the company, of whom divers were blasted.

The spectral hound then fled the church, leaving great scorch marks on the door as it scrambled its way out. Intriguingly enough, whilst the storm and the deaths (attributed to lightning striking the tower) are mentioned in the Parish Registry, there is no mention of The Dog. Even a year later when funds for repairs were being discussed there is still no mention of the Black Dog or the story. However, today the story is entrenched in local folklore and is a central part of the town's civic and cultural identity. The town is also now a favourite destination for crypto-zoologists, folklorists and those interested in the paranormal. Furthermore, the tale of the Black Dog of Bungay is far from isolated, with the legend of Black Shuck the fey Dog of Norfolk a central part of the mythology of the Broads. This story is paralleled in other local English mythologies as far afield as Cornwall and Yorkshire.

In Bungay itself he is reputed to haunt the graveyard at St. Mary's, the ruins of Bungay Castle and the path of Bigods Way. Rider Haggard, writing in the late nineteenth century also noted the Black Dog of Bungay was believed to haunt an area near the neighbouring town of Ditchingham called Hollow Hill.[2] As Chris Reeve, co-author of this book notes in his earlier work *A Straunge and Terrible Wunder*, the Black Dog is very much alive in local culture. The legend has helped to shape the identity of Bungay residents and children and the story is taught in the local schools. Many people believe they have encountered him in their wanderings around the Waveney Valley. The town is rife with symbolism and imagery of the Black Dog, from the town weather-vane, coat of arms and the Black Dog Marathon to numerous sporting clubs and shops and commemorative items. The mythology of the Black Dog is very much a living part of town identity and culture. Chris Reeve has an anecdote that is worth using to illustrate this point.

---

2   Haggard, R. *Farmer's Year: Being the Common Lore Book* for 1898. Longman Green & Co: New York, 1899. 26.

My niece, Charlotte, then aged 5 was taken to a flower festival in St. Mary's Church. One of the floral arrangements featured an image of the Black Dog, and as Charlotte was rather intrigued by it, her father narrated the story in some detail. That night she had a young friend to stay with her, and I had been asked to baby sit for them. Having tucked them up in bed and said goodnight, as I went downstairs I could hear Charlotte beginning to recount the story she had heard to her friend. Some time later, the sound of sobbing came from the room. On investigation, it became apparent that Charlotte had become so terrified while she was telling the story that she had burst into uncontrollable tears. I tried to comfort her, explaining that it had all happened hundreds of years ago and, in any case, 'it was only a story'. But she refused to be pacified, crying – 'But he's still alive – I saw him.' [3]

Similarly, on one of my own stays in Bungay visiting my parents, my father was minister of Emmanuel Church there at the time, my seven year old daughter had heard the story and after diligently searching the local mole-hills around St. Mary's had found a claw shaped stone which must have been the Black Dog's claw. This relieved her greatly as it meant that the Dog must be dead now as she had found its claws on a grave. However, she then thought there must have been more than one dog and its descendants could still be roaming around the town. After returning home to Australia she mentioned to me that her class-mates were not ready to deal with monsters being real, even if they lived far away in England, so she had refrained from discussing it in morning show-and-tell and had kept the claw secret. I relate these stories as a way of illustrating how rapidly stories enter the cultural framework of people and the vividness with which the folklore enters the imagination. The story continues to be a part of the public imagination in Bungay and as such becomes part of a common cultural tradition that is a central part of community spirit.

The purpose of this book is not to engage in a crypto-zoological or paranormal study of the Black Dog's attack on St. Mary's in 1577 but to look at the evolution of a local folklore in relation to the issues faced in a small, relatively isolated town over the centuries. From the Reformation to the English Civil War and to the Industrial Revolution, the town has experienced fire, civil unrest, religious turmoil, economic boom and bust, major demographic transformation and cultural change. As the town has

---

3   Reeve, Chris. *A Straunge and Terrible Wunder: The Story of the Black Dog of Bungay*. Peter Morrow and Co: Bungay, 1988. 2–3

been transformed through these events, so too has the culture and folklore of the community and this gives us great insight into the nature of local myths, community identity and culture.

It is in this respect that whilst there are numerous studies of Black Dog myths across the United Kingdom, and even globally, we have chosen to look at the story of the Black Dog of Bungay on its own as a case study of the evolution of local folklore. This decision was also made with an eye to a common critique of Black Dog studies. This will be discussed in more detail in Chapter 3, but briefly, there is a tendency of folklorists and mythologists to look at phenomena such as the Black Dog myths collectively in order to merge them together into one narrative of Black Dog mythology. This approach often glosses over important distinctions and differences between them and their specific local context and, whilst helpful in seeing the broader picture of mythology and archetypal representations of Black Dogs in folklore, it can also occlude as much as it reveals regarding the specific circumstance of an individual piece of folklore in its own communal and social context. Students of Black Dog myths and legends will undoubtedly see aspects which link to broader representations in folklore and mythology, as did Chris and I in producing this book; however, this study will focus specifically on the Black Dog of Bungay in its regional context in the Waveney Valley.

The Origins of the Black Dog Mythology

Dogs as guardians of the underworld, psychopomps and agents of the spirit world have a long history in human mythology and this history is far broader than that of the British Isles. Myths of Dogs foretelling death, standing vigil over graves, guiding people through the underworld and as fearsome supernatural threats originate in cultures as diverse as Nigeria and the pre-Hispanic Aztec Empire.[4] In the British Isles there is a rich body of mythology surrounding Black Dogs dating back to the Celts, the Roman Conquest and the Saxons. It forms a richly textured underlay behind Black Dog legends in post-Reformation Britain. Most studies of Black Dog folklore begin with a discussion of Anubis, the Egyptian Jackal headed god of death and judgement who guided lost souls to the underworld. Similarly, the Greek Dog Cerberus, often depicted with three heads and guarding

---

4   Ojade, J. O. 'Nigerian Cultural Attitudes to the Dog.' *Signifying Animals: Human Meaning in the Natural World*. Routledge: New York, 1990. 219; Burchell, S. *Phantom Black Dogs in Pre-Hispanic Mexico*. Heart of Albion Press: Loughborough, 2007. 1–8

the entrance to the underworld, is usually considered with its deep legacy in Saxon and later medieval classical studies. From this we can put forward the hypothesis that the Black Dog legend was brought to the British Isles by the Roman occupation. Conversely there existed an indigenous body of Black Dog mythology amongst the Celts, with the mythic figure of the Morrigan constructed as a goddess of death, war and carnage, appearing occasionally in the form of an enormous Black Hound or Raven. There are also the spectral hounds of the Cwn Annwn from Welsh mythology that guard the underworld and bring portent of death or disaster.

Clare Painting-Stubbs in her unpublished Masters thesis makes an argument for the folklore of the Black Dog of Bungay to have developed from the experience of the Viking conquests of East Anglia during the Sixth to Eighth centuries. She argues that from rather ambivalent representations of Black Dogs as psychopomps, guardians and guides of the underworld during the sixth to eighth centuries, Black Dogs became sinister figures of dread, actively seeking people out for misfortune and death. Investigating this change further she comes to the conclusion that the primary instigator of this change was the Viking invasion and colonization of much of the British Isles during this period. This is particularly represented by the areas most commonly associated with Black Dog folklore, East Anglia, Lincolnshire, Cornwall and Yorkshire. These are also the areas most heavily settled by Scandinavians and who suffered most heavily under Viking assaults.[5] In particular, she notes that there was a common cultural association of Viking assaults with the rapacious attack of wolves, as chronicled in the Annals of St. Bertin in the ninth century. Vikings were often labelled as dogs, as a form of abuse through the Old English term Hund, from which we derive the modern hound. Similarly, the term Wulf in Old English could mean literally a Wolf, but also a cruel person with se awyrgda wulf referring to the Devil. She also makes the argument that in Old English, Wulf and Dog were often used interchangeably; leading to a close association with the rapacious nature of Viking assaults and the death and destruction they wrought and the

5   This theory is paralleled by arguments made independently by Peter Jennings. Painting-Stubbs, C. *Religion, Familiars and Abraham Fleming: An Attempt to Explain the Strange and Terrible Wonder of 1577*. Submitted 21 September 2001, in fulfilment of a Masters Degree at the University of Kent. 5–8. Similarly, Barbara Allen Woods argues that the evidence is simply too sparse to make this kind of direct association with any kind of certainty. Woods, B. A. *The Devil in Dog Form: A Partial Type Index of Devil Legends*. University of California Press: Los Angeles, 1957. 2-3.

folklore of Dogs in general. This pattern is exacerbated by the use of war-dogs by Viking raiders, much like their Celtic counterparts 600 years earlier, and the common usage of Wolf symbolism in the Norse pantheon.[6]

Another important source of Black Dog mythology is the reclaiming of classical motifs, and medieval Christian representations of Black Dogs as symbolic of the Devil and his agents. Barbara Woods, in her dissertation on Faust, argued that the imagery originated out of an already established oral folklore of Black Dogs associated with the underworld and the Devil, and that Black Dog folklore was a widespread and vital tradition upon which numerous Devil legends and tales were based.[7] Whilst refraining from making claims to direct linear antecedents to Germanic folklore, she does focus on two streams of mythological traditions shaping these legends: both the Germanic folkloric traditions that are the basis of her study and the classical motifs appropriated into medieval Christian mythology.

In Latin literature Black Dogs play a strong theme in medieval folklore, remedies, rituals and mythology. Actual dogs, especially black dogs, played a wide variety of roles in rituals designed to heal sickness and injury. They were also routinely associated with omens of death and served as guardians of temples.[8] Similarly, the role of figures associated with Dogs and the underworld, like Cerberus and Hecate from classical studies, was well known by scholars of classical literature and would have also formed part of the background folklore of Black Dogs throughout the British Isles. Certainly a religious writer like Abraham Fleming would have been very familiar with both the popular folklore of his day and religious demonology, which will be discussed in more detail in the next chapter.

---

6   Painting-Stubbs, C. *Religion, Familiars and Abraham Fleming.* 7–8. It is worth noting that this view is critiqued by Mike Burgess who argues that Wolves and Dogs are quite distinct in Germanic mythology, there is no historical evidence for Thor possessing a hound called Shukr and whilst Odin had a pair of Wolves follow him into battle, they are quite peripheral to his Ravens Huginn and Muninn. Similarly, he also argues that the claim that Black Dog sightings are more common in areas of Viking settlement does not hold up to scrutiny given that phantom Black Dogs appear in areas uncontaminated by Viking beliefs. www.hiddenea.com/shuckland/mythconception2.htm also see Dale-Green, P. *Dog.* Hart-Davis: London, 1966.

7   Woods, B. A. *The Devil in Dog Form.* 1; Woods, Barbara Allen. 'The Devil in Dog Form.' *Western Folklore.* Vol 13. No 4. Oct 1954. 229–235.

8   Burris, E. 'The Place of the Dog in Superstition as Revealed in Latin Literature.' *Classical Philology.* Vol 30. No 1. Jan 1935. 32–42.

Stories like that of Bungay were not unprecedented. In 856 it is recorded that

> In August Teotogaundus, Bishop of Trier, with clerics and people was celebrating the office, when a very dreadful cloud, with thunderstorms and lightning, terrified the whole congregation in the church, and deadened the sound of bells ringing in the tower. The whole building was filled with such a dense darkness that one and another could hardly see or recognise his or her neighbour. On a sudden there was seen a dog of immense size (cano nimiae enormitas) in a sudden opening of the floor or earth (suito terrawe histu) and it ran to and fro around the altar.[9]

Similarly, John Stow records in 1538 that,

> My Father told me that, at St. Michaels Church in the Cornhill ward, London, on the night of St. James, certain men were ringing the bells of St. Michaels in the loft when there arose a tempest of thunder and lightning, and a thing of an ugly shape and sight was seen to come in at the south window, and it lighted on the North. For fear whereof, all of the ringers fell down and lay as dead for a time, leaving the bells to ring of their own accord. When the ringers came to themselves, they found certain stones of the north window to be raised and scat as if they had been so much butter, printed with a lions claw; the same stones were fastened there again, when it repaired, and remain so to this day. I have seen them oft and have put a feather or a small stick into the hole where the claw had entered, three of four inches deep. At the same time, certain timber postes at Queen hith were scat and cleft from top to bottom. And the pulpit cross in Paul's churchyard was likewise scratched cleft and overturned. One of the ringers lived in my youth, whom I have oft heard to verify the same to be true and I have oft heard my father to report it.[10]

Whilst we have a wide variety of sources to support folklore surrounding Black Dogs which would have been both familiar to Fleming and to the people of Bungay, it is difficult to assert any singular source to the story of

---

9   Certin, Fr. Historian living in 1160 wrote or compiled Annales Francorum Regum and was connected to the monastery of Sitheiu founded by St. Bertin 707AD at St. Omer (Pas de Calais) as recorded by Theo' Brown in the Theo' Brown Archives University of Exeter.

10   Stow, John writing of St. Michaels Cornhill c 1538. Recorded by Theo' Brown. Theo' Brown Archives University of Exeter.

the Black Dog, let alone a single origin or line of transmission to the present. It is even very difficult to show that there was a great deal of connection between the pamphlet written and published by Fleming in London and the people of Bungay themselves. As we will discuss in Chapter 3, there was a strong tendency in folklore studies to presume folklore, myths and legends of the rural parts of the British Isles represented isolated cultural fossils of a distant past. This approach assumed a culturally static unchanging countryside that represented a pure unadulterated authentic English culture uncorrupted by cosmopolitanism and industry. Similarly, folklore and ritual were often presented as pagan survivals of a primordial past which could be taken as powerful emotive links to a perceived uncontaminated Englishness.[11]

Even outside of romantic folklore studies there is a strong tendency to see the development of folklore as a linear progression of culture from the primordial past to the present. The Black Dog Institute into Depression Studies, for example, postulates that the use of the Black Dog as a euphemism of depression follows a linear cultural progress from prehistory through Roman and Greek culture to the Celts to the Black Dog of Bungay story and finally to Winston Churchill.[12]

Whilst the legacy of these ancient traditions certainly has a lasting impact on the mythology of Black Dogs and has certainly shaped the story of the Black Dog of Bungay, the transmission of folklore and mythology is far more complex than the legacy of pagan survivals would attest. A simple counterpoint to make to this theory is the presumption that if we are to claim Viking or Celtic origins for the tale, we would be presuming that experiences of hundreds of years ago would be of more significance than more recent cultural forms. Similarly, if we were to claim ancient origins we also have to deal with the fact that a sixteenth-century puritan in Bungay is unlikely to know what Anubis, Garm or even a Celt is. This is rendered more problematic by the fact that these symbols and images, far from being static culture fossils, are constantly in a state of transformation compounded by numerous discontinuities and retrospective reconstruction by various sectors of society throughout history in radically different social and cultural contexts.

---

11   These issues will be dealt with in detail in chapters 3 and 4.

12   Hanley, Sue. 'The Black Dog Mystery' www.blackdoginstitute.org.au/docs/ Hanley.pdf

Folklore

Folklore as a concept and a discipline, as we will discuss in Chapter 3, emerged out of an anxiety surrounding the death of tradition in the aftermath of the Industrial Revolution. As a consequence there is a strong tendency to look to folkloric practices, rituals and legends as vehicles necessary to come to terms with heritage. That being said, the social function of folklore is rooted deeply in the lived social and cultural world of people in a living ever changing community. So in this sense, whilst there are always legacies of past ideas, symbols and images in any cultural form, it is a mistake to assume a linear progression of tradition in any kind of stasis from the past. Even in a legend or belief which can be traced back to antiquity, the meaning and significance of the cultural form will change in relation to experiences of the community that practice it. Fixation on the past as a source of authenticity in culture is itself a product of contemporary cultural anxieties during the Industrial Revolution. This can often lead to unfortunate judgements of the legitimacy of ritual, belief and symbolism according to ideological presuppositions quite alien to the cultures being studied. There is also, as we will discuss in detail in Chapters 3 and 4, a powerful self perpetuating myth, where the very act of researching and publishing theories of folklore in popular and academic press, shapes the context through which people make sense of their own traditions and rituals. This is particularly evident in the retelling of Black Dog of Bungay tale which has been very strongly influenced by various popular and academic interpretations of the legend from other sources around the world.

Similarly, legitimacy in folklore is not defined by empirical accuracy in the sense of the modern historian, though, in a post-enlightenment world the claim to historical accuracy may be a source of anxiety to belief, ritual and symbolism.[13] Professor Ronald Hutton, for example, describes the frustration of the modern historian trying to utilise folklore as the basis of empirical research in great detail in his book *Witches, Druids and King Arthur*, perhaps best represented by the line 'once a fiction is crafted cleverly enough to provide an entertaining story, it has the capacity to overpower virtually any facts given sufficient time.'[14] This is not to say that folklore is arbitrarily defined by popular culture but there are very clearly rules within

---

13 For an example of the impact of this anxiety surrounding empirical accuracy in folk belief in relation to the legacy of Pagan survivals I recommend my book, Waldron, David. *The Sign of the Witch: Modernity and the Pagan Revival*. Carolina Academic Press: Durham, 2008. 202–218

14 Hutton, R. *Witches, Druids and King Arthur*. Hambledon Continuum: New York, 2003. 12

the structure of the folklore of a particular community which govern the significance of these representations. They are shaped by a wide variety of issues, as will be illustrated through this book. In this context I would add to Hutton's comment above the addendum of whether the fiction is of sufficient utility and cultural resonance to the community. As Hutton indicates, two particularly pertinent issues which shape this process of folkloric constructions of the past are firstly, the tendency for the past to be transformed into an object of utility to the present and secondly, the reshaping of memories and transmission of the past in a community through later profound or traumatic experiences.[15]

Folklore, as defined by Jan Harold Brunwald, is the culture of the unofficial, traditional and non-institutionalised part of culture. It encompasses the knowledge, values, symbols, feelings, beliefs and concepts transmitted by word of mouth, popular art, music and other forms of local social exchange.[16] In this sense, one of the central functions of folklore is communication within communities and, as such, the context in which the people of that community find themselves forms the central basis in which the expression of folklore has meaning. Each community has its own structures of communication, belief, rituals and symbols that contain forms which both bear reference to the past and the experiences of that community over time and the contemporaneous context in which they find themselves in the present.

In this sense folklore is much like a language. It serves as the basis of shared cultural heritage, communication of meaning and transmission of ideas within a community. The meaning of these cultural forms is intrinsically contextual in relation to the social, economic and cultural issues facing that community. Meaning in folklore is also constructed out of diverse fragments of symbolism, narrative and ritual in much the same way that we construct meaning in verbal communication. To take this analogy further, in relation to language, in English, for example, there are many fragments of words of which some may be of immense antiquity: there are remnants of Gaelic, Saxon and Latin dialects in many of our modern words. While we may use these words freely in communication and the legacy of the history that these words come from has a significant influence on our culture and identity, it does not mean that we are either conscious of their antecedents

---

15   Hutton, R. *Witches, Druids and King Arthur.* 21

16   Brunwald, J. *The Study of American Folklore: An Introduction.* 4th Ed. Warton: New York. 1998. 4

in our use of these terms, nor does it mean that they have the same meaning in today's communication as they did in their original context. So, like language, whilst there may be fragments of symbols, rituals, language and ideas from antiquity circulating around an object of contemporary folklore like the Black Dog of Bungay, it does not mean that people in the sixteenth century were conscious of or interpreted it in the context of Germanic or Celtic myth. Nor does it mean that any one particular antecedent is more true than another in trying to make sense of these legacies in a contemporary context, any more than one could claim a sentence in modern English is really Latin, Gaelic or Saxon despite having potential antecedents in all three languages.

Collective memories are social and cultural constructs and their legacy is determined by their emotional importance and cultural resonance within the culture that experienced them. The transmission of ideas and the way they are interpreted is closely linked to the context in which they are told and interpreted. Similarly, the method by which these memories are transmitted has a great deal of impact on their legacy. The transmission of oral story-telling, for example, has a cultural resonance and structure quite distinct to visual art or a dance at a festival. Rumour, hearsay or pure aesthetic beauty can have an impact as strong, if not stronger than empirically accurate or authorized accounts. In this light the retrospective reconstruction of the past, even if long forgotten, can within a generation become an immutable continual link to the distant past in the minds of the people who have adopted it, as illustrated in the deliberate popularizing or repopularization of the Black Dog story in the 1930s, as we will see in Chapter 4.

This book, as a case study in the development of local folklore, is as much a study of the town of Bungay since the Reformation as it is a study of the Black Dog itself. As we have seen, a piece of folklore like the Black Dog of Bungay cannot be studied in isolation from the society that produced it and continues to develop it in the context of lived experience in the town of Bungay itself and, more recently, in globalized popular culture. There is a very complex pattern at work in the continued development of this folklore, between the community that spawned it, academic discourse on the topic, and broader exposure to popular culture, all of which continue to shape the mythology and the role the legend plays in local folklore. Even more important is the extent to which the legend itself was a product of intense community conflict common to much of England during the Reformation in which the local Catholic community was largely forced into hiding.

Similarly, the mythology re-emerged during the trauma of economic hardship and social transformation wrought by the Industrial Revolution and later the economic turmoil of the Great Depression.

This book is both a case study in the evolution of a local myth with a significant legacy in popular culture and it is the story of an English town and its community's attempts to come to terms with shared trauma and the transformation of daily life since the Reformation in local culture.

1

A Straunge and Terrible Wunder

The like thing entered, in the same shape and similitude where placing himself on a maine balke or beam whereon sometime the rood did stand, sodainly he gave a swing downe though the Church, and there also, as before, slew two men and a lad, and burned the hand of another person that was among the rest of the company, of whom divers were blasted.

– Abraham Fleming: *A Straunge and Terrible Wunder*

Woodcut from the reprint of Abraham Fleming's pamphlet published by T. & H. Rodd in 1826

The original tale of the Black Dog assaulting St. Mary's and its congregation is sourced, as stated in the introduction, almost entirely from the pamphlet of Abraham Fleming entitled a 'Straunge and Terrible Wunder wrought very late in the parish church of Bongay' which was published within a month after the events described in August of 1577. It was produced as a twelve page pamphlet on 9 x 15cm paper designed to be easily distributed and cheap to produce. Essentially it reads as a tabloid/

propaganda piece describing in dramatic lurid tones the thunderstorm that severely damaged the steeples of the Churches of Holy Trinity Blythburgh and St. Mary's Bungay combined with an assault by the Black Dog (or the Devil in such a likeness) on the church and parishioners in those towns as they assembled for morning worship. The pamphlet also featured an image of the Dog on the front cover as a crude wood-cut print of a dog like beast.

St. Mary's Church, Bungay

The account of the Black Dog, or 'the Devil in such a likeness', appearing in Bungay and Blythburgh churches in 1577, appears to have been an invention of Abraham Fleming (who gained the title Reverend some time after these events in 1588). No other extant contemporary accounts mention a black dog. The closest is an almost word for word translation of a pamphlet in France entitled Histoire Mervelleuse published the following year by Roland Jenkes a fervent Catholic printer living in exile in France who altered the ending of the pamphlet to represent a Catholic rather than Protestant point of view.17 Outside of the Fleming pamphlet and subsequent reprints, depictions of the August 4 event attribute the deaths and injuries and the

17   PhD transcript by Clare Stubbs at the University of Kent citing R.B. McKerrow (ed) *A Dictionary of Printers and Booksellers in England, Scotland and Ireland, and of Foreign Printers of English Books.* Martino Press: London, 1968. 156

damage to the churches as caused by lightning strikes during a devastating thunderstorm. Yet, despite this it is Fleming's version which has captured the public's imagination, and, nearly 450 years later continues to be one of the most popular of British folk legends. Why should this be so, and what significance did this pamphlet have for local people in the wake of the August 4 storm and the social turmoil of the religious Reformation in which it occurred?

Interior of St. Mary's Church, Bungay

Before these questions can be answered, an analysis of Fleming's pamphlet with its unique focus on a Satanic beast, an assessment of how his narrative compares with other contemporary records must be considered. The thunderstorm that precipitated the event was so remarkable that it is well documented in contemporary records. The Chronicles of England, Scotland, and Ireland, produced by Raphael Holinshed, a London printer, in 1578, and updated in 1586, published the following account for the year 1577:

> On Sunday, the fourth of August between the hours of nine and ten of the clock in the forenoon, whilst the minister was reading of the second lesson in the parish church of Bliborough (Blythburgh), a town in Suffolk, a strange and terrible tempest of lightning and thunder struck through the wall of the same church into the ground a yard deep, drew down all the people on that side, above twenty persons, then renting the wall up to the vestry, cleft the door, and returning to the steeple, rent the timber, broke the chimes, and fled towards Bungay, a town six miles off.

The people that were stricken down were found grovelling more than half an hour after, whereof one man more than forty years, and a boy of fifteen years old, were found stark dead; the others were scorched. The same or the like flash of lightning and cracks of thunder rent the parish church of Bungay, nine miles from Norwich, wrung in sunder the wires and wheels of the clocks, slew two men which sat in the belfry, when the others were at the procession of suffrages, and scorched another, which hardly escaped...

Holy Trinity Church, Blythburgh

This account contains explicit detail such as the time of the occurrence, the precise damage, the ages of the victims. It suggests that the information was provided by members of the congregation who were eye-witnesses of the event. Some of the information is confirmed by Blythburgh parish records which give information about repairs to the building, while the door with its scorch marks thought to have been caused by the lightning strikes still survives in situ.

The parish records of St. Mary's Church, Bungay, also confirm Holinshed's account and provide further detail. The Churchwardens' Register of Accounts for the year 1577 record:

Item: paid to the four poor women that laid forth the bodies of the two men that were stricken dead both within the steeple of the church at the great tempest that was on the 4th of August, 1577 . . . viiid (eight pence)

In the margin, the clerk has added: 'A great, terrible and fearful tempest at the time of the Procession upon the Sunday. Such darkness, rain, hail thunder & lightning as was never seen the like.'

Door of Holy Trinity Church, Blythburgh, showing the scorch marks caused by the Black Dog's flaming claws.

The Parish Burial Register provides the names of the two men who were killed:

> *John Fuller and Adam Walker, slain in the Tempest in the Belfry in the time of prayer upon the Lord's Day the 4th of August, 1577.*

In the margin, somebody has added: 'THE TEMPEST OF THUNDER'

Two years later, in 1579, the Churchwardens' Accounts Register mentions repairs to the church in the wake of the storm:

> Item: Paid to a carpenter for seven days work, with meat and wages, for mending and repairing the chyngling (glazing bars) of the steeple window at the east side, that was broken and jagged in pieces at the great tempest of thunder and lightning that was at Bungay the 4th of August, being Sunday, in AD 1577, when two of the parishioners were stricken dead in the Bellhouse, and died, some others of the parishioners stricken down to the ground, and some hurt in diverse places of their legs and feet, to the great fears of all the parishioners.

The event was still so terrifyingly vivid in everyone's mind, that there is another marginal comment: '1577, 4th of August, being Sunday, such thunder, lightning, rain and darkness as never was seen the like. Never to be forgotten.'

All these accounts provide similar information, and, were it not for the testimony of the Reverend Abraham Fleming, the event would have been all but forgotten, recalled only by local historians as an interesting footnote in Bungay and Blythburgh church history.

Fleming is thought to have been born in London in about 1552,[18] and was a student at Cambridge University about twenty years later, although he did not graduate until 1582. He was ordained priest, and served as a private chaplain to Lord Howard of Effingham, and was perhaps also employed as a tutor before becoming Rector of St. Pancras church, in Soper Lane, London, in 1593. He died in 1607, whilst staying with his brother at Bottesford in Leicestershire. He was a prolific author, publishing a variety

---

18   In her doctoral thesis, Clare Painting-Stubbs argues that he is more likely to have been born in about 1547–48 whereas the memorial plaque in Bottesford Church, Leicestershire, where he was buried, states that he was about 56 when he died in 1607.

of works, and became an editor of the new edition of the Holinshed's Chronicles in 1586 for which he may well have provided the account of the Bungay and Blythburgh thunderstorms.

The Anglican Church was predominantly Protestant at this period and had a tendency for promoting 'hellfire and damnation' sermons and tracts, emphasizing the need for redemption and virtue, or else a wrathful God would inflict terrible punishments upon sinners. Fleming seems to have been of Calvinist tendency, that is one who supported the religious doctrines of John Calvin, and advocated a stricter form of Protestant theology and worship than was congenial to some sections of the Reformed Church. Holinshed probably shared a similar view, which may be one reason why he employed him as a contributor to the Chronicles, which in 1574, described a thunderstorm in much the same language that Fleming would later use in his 1577 Bungay pamphlet:

> At night blew very stormy and tempestuous winds out of the south, as hath not been known the like out of that quarter. . . . These are to be received as token's of God's wrath ready bent against the world for sin now abounding . . . who doeth only thus but to show us the rod wherewith we daily deserve to be beaten.

As far as is known, Fleming was not connected with Suffolk, and never visited Bungay or Blythburgh. It seems likely that, having heard about the thunderstorm in London, where he is thought to have been resident at the time, he decided to elaborate the account and publish it as a tract. This would not only exemplify his Protestant views, and promote himself as a God-fearing priest seeking preferment in the church, but also earn him some useful extra income.

The pamphlet would obviously sell better if the contents were made as sensational as possible, which is how modern newspaper journalism still operates today. The event was terrifying enough, involving severe damage to two of God's temples, several deaths and awful injuries caused by scorching. But it could attract even more publicity, and sales, if another dimension was added, that of attributing the cause not to a thunderstorm, but to God's adversary Satan himself. And in this case it was Satan in the disguise of a savage Black Dog, perhaps one of the types already described in Fleming's translation from the Latin of John Caius 'Of English Dogges' published in 1576.

The pamphlet was consequently issued shortly after the event occurred, for Fleming affirms in his Preface that 'the terror of the same is at this instant freshe in memorie'. Its title page, in typical journalistic style, was designed to immediately attract interest and curiosity:

> A Straunge and Terrible Wunder, wrought very late in the Parish Church of Bongay, a Town of no great distance from the citie of Norwich, namely the fourth of this August, in ye yeere of our Lord 1577, in a great tempest of violent raine, lightning, and thunder, the like of which hath been seldome seen.

> With the appearance of an horrible shaped thing, sensibly perceived of the people then and there assembled.

> Drawen into a plain method according to the written copy by Abraham Fleming.

He goes on to address the reader in true Protestant polemical style with the real substance of his message: that the Bungay event was a timely warning, 'A spectacle no doubt of God's judgement, which as the fire of our iniquities hath kindled, so, by none other meanes then by the teares of repentance may it bee quenched.'

The main part of Fleming's narrative is similar to the descriptions already quoted, commencing with the occurrence of the storm, and describing the deaths, injuries and damage that resulted. It differs in introducing the supernatural element of the Black Dog, and making it the instrument of the disaster. It also focuses primarily on the event in Bungay, with Blythburgh given a secondary role, and allocated only a single paragraph of the complete narrative. Why this should be so is unclear, but it may be that Fleming received more direct and detailed information from Bungay informants which could create a more colourful story for his readers.

Having described the storm as taking place between nine and ten o'clock on the Sunday morning, and emphasizing its unnatural fury, he goes on to recount what happened in St. Mary's Church:

> There were assembled at the same season, to hear divine service and common prayer, according to order, in the parish church of the said towne of Bongay, the people thereabouts inhabiting, who were witnesses of the straungenes, the rarenesse and sodenesse of the storm, consisting of raine violently falling, fearful flashes of lightning, and terrible cracks of thunder, which came with such unwonted force and power, that to the perceiving

of the people, at the time and in the place above named, assembled, the Church did as it were shake and stagger, which struck into the harts of those that were present, such a sore and sodain feare, that they were in a manner robbed of their right wits.

Immediately hereupon, there appeared in a most horrible similitude and likenesse to the congregation then and there present, a dog as they might discerne it, of a black colour; at the sight whereof, together with the fearful flashes of fire which then were seene, moved such admiration in the mindes of the assemblie, that they thought Doomes day was already come.

This black dog, or the Devil in such a likenesse (God hee knoweth all who worketh all), running all along down the body of the church with great swiftnesse and incredible haste, among the people, in a visible form and shape, passed between two persons, as they were kneeling upon their knees, and occupied in prayer as it seemed, wrung the necks of them bothe clene backward, in somuch that even at a moment where they kneeled, they strangely died.

There was at ye same time another wonder wrought: for the same black dog, still continuing and remaining in one and the self same shape, passing by another man of the congregation in the church, gave him such a gripe on the back, that therewith all he was presently drawen together and shrunk up, as it were a piece of leather scorched in a hot fire; or as the mouth of a purse or bag, drawen together with a string. The man, albeit he was in so straunge a taking, dyed not, but as it is thought is yet alive: whiche thing is mervelous in the eyes of men, and offereth muche matter of amasing the minde.

Moreover, and beside this, the Clark of the said Church, being occupied in cleansing of the gutter of the church, with a violent clap of thunder was smitten downe, and beside his fall had no further harme: unto whom being all amased this straunge shape, whereof we have before spoken, appeared, howbeit he escaped without daunger: which might peradventure seem to sound against truth, and to be a thing incredible: but, let us leave thus or thus to judge, and cry out with the Prophet, O Domine, &c. – O Lord, how wonderful art thou in thy works!

Fleming goes on to provide what he believes is evidence for his remarkable story: —

> As testimonies and witnesses of the force which rested in this strange shaped thing, there are remaining in the stones of the Church, and likewise in the Church door which are marvellously reten and torne, ye marks as it were of his clawes or talons. Beside, that all the wires, the wheeles, and other things belonging to the Clock, were wrung in sunder, and broken in pieces.
>
> And, (which I should have tolde you in the beginning of this report, if I had regarded the observing of order)at the same time that this tempest lasted, and while these storms endured, ye whole Churche was so darkened, yea, with such a palpable darknesse, that one persone could not perceive another, neither yet might discern any light at all, thought it were lesser than the least, but onely when ye great flashing of fire and lightning appeared.

He concludes with a brief account of the similar disaster at Blythburgh:

> On the self same day, in like manner, into the parish church of another town called Blibery (sic), not above seven miles distant from Bungay above said, the like thing entered, in the same shape and similitude, where placing himself upon a maine balke or beam, whereon sometime ye Rood did stand, sudainly he gave a swinge down through ye church, and there also, as before, slew two men and a lad, & burned the hand of another person that was there among the rest of the company, of whom divers were blasted.
>
> This mischief thus wrought, he flew with wonderful force to no little feare of the assembly, out of the church in a hideous and hellish likeness.
>
> These things are reported to be true, yea, by the mouthes of them that were eye witnesses of the same, and therefore dare with so much the more boldenesse verifie what soever is reported.
>
> Let us pray unto God, as it is the dutie of Christians, to work all things to the best, to turne our flintie hearts into fleshlie hearts, that we may feele the fire of God's mercy, and flee from the scourge of his justice.

The pamphlet concludes with 'A Necessary Prayer', beseeching God, that

> although we, through the infinite and unmeasurable sinnes whiche we commit, provoke thee to smite us with the Iron rod of thy wrath and

judgement: yet that it would please thee to remember that we are but fraile flesh, subject to sinne, & too prone to offend: that it would please thee to cast thy gratious countenance upon us, and to stretch out thy silvered sceptre of peace unto us, that being restored into thy favour from whiche our offences have separated us, we may shrowd our selves under the shield of thy safegarde against all manner of annoyances whatsoever, through Christ Jesus our onely Savior & Redeemer, in whose name, as hee hath taught us, we say and pray . . . Deliver us from all evil, good Lord, Amen.

This epitaph is typical of the preaching of the period, and may well have formed the conclusion of a similar sermon delivered from the pulpit, by the Bungay vicar, in the days following the terrible disaster.

Leaving aside, for the time being, the introduction of the beastly protagonist of the disaster, the main departure from the other recorded accounts of the event is that Fleming describes the deaths and injuries at Bungay as occurring in the nave where the congregation was assembled for morning worship, whereas it is clear from the Bungay parish records that only two men in the church belfry were killed. From Fleming's point of view it made the narrative much more dramatic if the disaster struck at the very heart of the congregation, particularly as he saw the Black Dog's presence as a punishment for sin. It would have been difficult for him to explain why two men separated from the rest of the congregation in the belfry should be particularly singled out for God's wrath. He would then have to explain why they deserved their fate more than any others. The whole thrust of his polemic is that the entire congregation of the parish was targeted, and those that were wounded and killed were to serve as a warning to all the others who were witnesses.

It needs to be pointed out that the two men who were killed, Adam Walker and John Fuller, had almost certainly rushed up into the belfry as soon as the thunderstorm occurred to ring the bells in order to frighten away the evil spirits in the atmosphere that were believed to be responsible for thunder and lightning in the superstitious Tudor period. Thunderstorms were greatly feared at a time when most houses were built of timber and thatch. A lightning strike could easily set a thatch ablaze which could then spread like wildfire to all the adjoining properties. Unfortunately, they were in the wrong place at the wrong time: the tower was struck by lightning, and the two men were killed. The parish records make it clear that the tower suffered the most damage, which is why people assembled in the nave got off comparatively lightly with only burns caused by the lightning strikes: 'stricken down to the ground & some hurt in diverse places of their legs and feet', as the Churchwardens' Registers reported in 1579.

The people of Bungay all knew that only two of their neighbours in the belfry had been killed. When they read or heard about Fleming's pamphlet they would surely be enraged to discover that it was providing untrue information, just as the public gets annoyed today when tabloid newspapers report sensational news items exaggerated out of all proportion. And the belfry deaths also contradict Fleming's assertion that his account was based on eye-witness reports. There are unlikely to have been any eye-witnesses to the deaths of Walker and Fuller, and their horribly scorched and crushed remains would only have been discovered some time after the storm had subsided.

If no credence could be given locally to the accuracy of Fleming's text, at least as far as the Bungay narrative was concerned, criticisms must have spread. They might have been reported to the church authorities, and presumably reached Fleming's ears eventually. This could explain why in later accounts, for example, in Holinshed's Chronicles, the story omits the reference to the deaths in the nave, and only mentions the belfry mortalities. Unfortunately, any contemporary Blythburgh parish records do not survive, so it is not known how accurately Fleming reported the event in Holy Trinity church, but the news that he had allegedly lied about the Bungay story would cast doubts on all other aspects of the pamphlet. This may also explain why the Bungay story is given less prominence in the Chronicles. The editors may have felt that it had been discredited, and it was therefore better to concentrate on the supposedly more truthful report concerning the Blythburgh thunderstorm.

Similarly, as Fleming had misrepresented the truth with regard to the fatalities, his tale about the Black Dog could also be viewed as a complete fabrication. Some contemporaries may have poured scorn on the sensational elements of a story clearly designed to increase sales to benefit himself and his printers. In fact it appears that Fleming may have suffered some legal difficulties over the writing and promotion of the pamphlet given that the Acts of the Privy Council record that,

Unlicensed Publications: A letter to the Bishop of London signifienge unto him that where there hathe been latelie published to (two) pamphlettes, the one concerning a straing accident sade to have happened within the parish church of Bongy, neere unto Norwich.[19]

However, there is perhaps more to this story than simple manipulative and lurid Calvinist propaganda. In his account, he firmly states that his information was 'reported to be true, yea, by the mouthes of them that were eye witnesses of the same'. In this light he seems to be claiming that what he is reporting is accurate representation of what eye-witnesses reported to him and thus errors in reporting are a product of his witnesses rather than his own faithful reporting of their tale. There is certainly the possibility he wrote what he had been told by witnesses or through hearsay and only later found people disputed his version of events, hence the much more circumspect representation of the storm in the Chronicle. Similarly, he seems to have published his pamphlet with extraordinary haste, perhaps before more accurate information had had time to filter through. That might explain why the versions of the story are differently reported in the Chronicles.

Before analysing what he means by his term 'eye-witnesses' it is necessary to make a few comments about his sometimes ambivalent use of language in the text. It seems odd, for example, that in the introduction to the pamphlet he does not describes the malevolent beast as a dog but as 'an horrible shaped thing, sensibly perceived of the people then and there assembled'. There is a huge difference between 'horrible-shaped thing' and a dog. It is quite likely that the congregation could imagine some horrible shaped presence in the darkness of the church which was lit only by occasional flashes of violent lightning. Seeing a dog is something much more definite. It suggests that Fleming may have phrased it in this vague way, because he was aware that he could be criticised for providing false information.

It is true that the cover of his pamphlet depicts a wood-cut of an animal, rather than a 'thing', but, as Clare Painting-Stubbs suggests, this image may only have been used because the printer happened to have it amongst his printing blocks. Also, it has to be said that it does not look a lot like a dog. It is more like a small bear with a stringy tail, or a sheep with claws. It does not even look fierce or frightening, but might just pass muster as 'an horrible shaped thing'. From our rational and scientific modern day viewpoint it is much easier to believe that a frightened and superstitious congregation believed they imagined a 'horrible shaped thing' amongst them, than that they actually saw a black dog: and some of the language Fleming uses seems

---

19   Dasent, J. R. (ed.) *Acts of the Privy Council of England*, Vol. X, A.D. 1577–1578. London: HMSO, 1895. 25.

to support this interpretation. That being said the main body of the text quickly progresses to a representation of an enormous Black Dog.[20]

Fleming adds that when the storm commenced, the congregation 'were in a manner robbed of their right wits.' Can any faith be put in the accuracy of statements by those who are temporarily deranged? Furthermore, he does not assert at this point that there was a dog, but only 'in a most horrible similitude and likenesse to the congregation . . . a dog as they might discerne it'. Once again the language is cautious: robbed of their 'right wits', did they see a dog or not? Did they instead see 'an horrible shaped thing', or just scary and blinding flashes of lighting, making their eyes see all sorts of strange shapes and colours?

Fleming goes on to mention the clerk who was outside in the churchyard clearing the gutters, and who is not mentioned in any of the other accounts. Fleming says that 'straunge shape', the Black Dog, appeared before him, and as nobody else would have been outside at the time, it sounds like a real eye-witness account, a personal testimony from the clerk himself. If so there is no other evidence to corroborate it, and so must be viewed with a degree of caution, although it is certainly possible that Fleming's other 'eye-witnesses' may have reported what the clerk told them after the event. In fact the role of cleaning the gutters would normally be the responsibility of the verger, who is frequently referred to in the parish accounts. Fleming seems vague about such details, but that is not surprising if he was relying on local gossip. The role of the clerk would normally be to write the accounts in the parish registers. If it really was the clerk who witnessed the 'straunge shape', he certainly does not mention such an occurrence in his entries.

Fleming is similarly lacking in accurate information when he goes on to mention how the minister of the church 'being partaker of the people's perplexitie, seeing what was seen, and done, comforted the people, and exhorted them to prayer'. He is keen to suggest greater veracity in his account by adding in the clergyman as an eye-witness, but he does not know whether he is a Rector or a Curate, or even his name (in fact incumbents of St. Mary's parish were more usually Vicars). This suggests that the information he received was scanty, and that he did not bother to get in touch with the priest to find out what had actually happened, as any reliable investigative reporter would do today. The priest in charge must obviously be a

---

20 It is worth noting that many of the representations of Black Dogs in folklore recorded during the nineteenth century refer to shape-changing supernatural creatures which can take the form of a Black Dog but can appear in other forms as well such as a shapeless mass which can change its form at will. See Chapter 4 for more discussion.

key eye-witness and his account is essential to understanding exactly what occurred. It further indicates that Fleming was much more interested in pointing the moral of the story, rather than providing a factual report of the event itself. His pamphlet could also have been subsequently discredited by the Bungay priest, who is likely to have been Robert Belye, newly appointed in that same year of 1577.[21]

However, it is a mistake to evaluate the kinds of reporting and story telling of the Tudor period by modern standards. At the very least, communication in the Tudor period was difficult and slow. Contacting the Bungay priest would have necessitated either sending a letter by a servant on horseback, or by coach, which, from London would be a distance of about 200 miles there and back, and incredibly slow on the rough unmade roads, taking five or six days. And Fleming, was keen to get his pamphlet issued as quickly as possibly before the sensational story was taken up by some other writer, thus ruining its novelty. As an ambitious young writer seeking to make a name for himself, speed was of the essence, and is entirely understandable in the circumstances. Clare Painting-Stubbs notes in her research, that he was reported to have said constantly that he had to work to make money. But the points touched upon cast grave doubts on the accuracy of his reporting, in terms of understanding the veracity of the Black Dog story.

In addition to what can be claimed as the evidence of eye-witnesses, Fleming introduces more tangible evidence which he believed could be seen by anybody visiting the building where the disaster happened. He states that as 'testimonie and witnesse of the force which rested in this strange shaped thing' (once again he hesitates in calling it a dog), is that there are

'remaining in the stones of the Church, and likewise in the Church dore which are marvellously reten and torne, ye marks, as it were, of his clawes or talons. Beside, that all the wires, the wheeles, and other things belonging to the Clock, were wrung in sunder, and broken to pieces.'

Some of this information also cannot be verified. It is likely that burn marks resulting from the lightning strikes affected both the Bungay St. Mary's, and Holy Trinity Church at Blythburgh. However, whereas the door of Blythburgh Church remains in situ, and exhibits what appear to be burn marks which could have been caused by lightning flashes, much of St. Mary's Church was severely damaged by the Great Fire of 1688. The

---

21   Mann, E. *Old Bungay*. Heath Cranton Ltd: London, 1933. 46.

raging fire would probably have left the stone-built fabric untouched, but in their terror, local people dragged bits of their burning furniture and other possessions, into the building for safety, and, as a result, set the church ablaze as well. It was severely damaged, and the tower and south aisle had to be rebuilt. It is likely that the porch door was also destroyed, and the existing door is a replacement. It contains central studded panels which might date back to the sixteenth century and have been reused, but if so, these have no burn marks similar to those in the Blythburgh door. Also, there is now no evidence of any 'clawes or talons' in the stones of the church. Storm damage was almost certainly evident at the time, however, and could by the superstitious be attributed to supernatural forces, and the damage to the clock is well attested in the parish records.

Rear view of St. Mary's Church, Bungay

Fleming makes what can again be interpreted as justification for his Black Dog theme, by stating that at the time of the event 'ye whole Church was so darkened, yea, with such a palpable darknesse, that one personne could not perceive another, neither yet might discerne any light at all, though it were lesser than the least, but onely when ye great flashing of fire and lighting appeared.' So it is clear that whatever the parishioners did see could only have been seen momentarily in the few seconds that it took the lightning to illuminate the interior. As they were in darkness, any sudden bright light would be more blinding than illuminating, and from our modern viewpoint, it seems likely that nothing as definite as a dog could be seen at all.

So Fleming seeks to exonerate himself from criticism, because he can always assert, if cross-examined, that the circumstances were so extreme that his 'eye-witnesses' could have been confused and mistaken. That being so, he is also careful not to dilute the sensationalism of his sermon by concluding with their testimony: 'These things are reported to be true, yea, by the mouthes of them that were eye-witnesses of the same, and therefore dare with so much the more boldenesse verifie what soever is reported.'

In true polemical style, he seems to be confidently affirming that his extraordinary narrative will be believed and marvelled over by all his readers.

The credibility of Fleming's version rests essentially upon the evidence of the 'eye-witnesses' he refers to. It has already been pointed out that he probably had little knowledge of Bungay, Blythburgh and the Suffolk area involved, and did not even know the role or name of the parish incumbents, nor can he name any of the 'eye-witnesses'. In his account the thunder-storm and lightning strikes are inextricably woven with the involvement of a supernatural Hell-hound, so it is necessary to try to distinguish between what the parishioners are likely to have seen and experienced, and what can only be conjectured.

The only 'eye-witnesses' were the parishioners who were assembled in the Bungay church for morning service at about nine or ten a.m. on that fateful morning. They experienced the church being plunged in darkness due to the storm clouds, the outbreak of the thunder and lightning and the lightning strikes on the building. They may not have been immediately aware of the damage caused to the belfry and the clock, and the smashing of the steeple window on the east side, but they may have heard the sounds of the impact as the lightning struck the tower high above them. They certainly witnessed the impact of the lightning as it struck the nave where they were assembled, and would have heard the screams and groans of agony as their relatives and neighbours were burned and injured, 'stricken down to the grounde & some hurt in diverse places of their leggs and feet to ye great feares of all ye parishioners'.[22] They could not have known about the deaths of John Fuller and Adam Walker in the belfry until sometime after the storm had subsided and their bodies were discovered. The full extent of the disaster could not be assessed until after the storm had subsided, when information could be gained about who had suffered injuries, who had been killed, and where and to what extent the church fabric was damaged.

---

22   St. Mary's Churchwardens' Registers, Lowestoft R.O.

This is what can be affirmed with some degree of confidence concerning what the 'eye-witnesses' experienced. But what does Fleming mean by 'eye-witnesses'? The tone of the text suggests that he may just have heard various and general reports about what had happened, and not directly from those who had been involved. His description of their experiences – their 'amasing and singular astonishment', 'perplexed in minde and at their wits end', their 'sore and sudden feare' which 'robbed them of their right wits' could be entirely imaginary, based upon how people would normally be expected to feel and react in such situations. He does conclude by emphatically affirming that, 'These things are reported to be true, yea, by the mouthes of them that were eye witnesses of the same', but as he does not mention any of them by name nor describe how and where he obtained the information it is quite likely that his sources were more indirect than he seems to be suggesting. The reports may have been second or third hand and are likely to have become garbled in the re-telling. And this contrasts with the parish records where what is reported must clearly have come from those people directly involved, and includes some description of the injuries suffered, which Fleming does not mention in his Bungay account.

His description of the injured man in Bungay who 'shrunk up, as it were a piece of leather scorched in a hot fire' does sound more like first hand experience, but if, so it seems odd that Fleming makes no mention of other injuries which could have enhanced the sensationalism of his story. It could be that he was relying on his own knowledge or imagination for this detail, or that this particular incident was actually reported to him, but not necessarily by an 'eye-witness'. His account of the experience of the thunderstorm, and the experience of the Black Dog are so interwoven, that it could be argued that what his 'witnesses' perceived was simply the storm and its effects, not necessarily the involvement of a dog. Yet he does seem at pains to affirm in his first mention of the dog that it 'appeared in a most horrible similitude and likenesse to the congregation then and there present.' Similarly, towards the end of his Blythburgh account, when he describes the Black Dog as flying 'in a hideous and hellish likenesse' out of the church, he firmly states that 'These things are reported to be true, yea, by the mouthes of them that were eye-witnesses of the same.' So, despite the ambiguity of the phrases and information he provides elsewhere in the tract, he is, in other paragraphs firmly asserting that what the congregations saw, and believed to be responsible was a Black Dog, or 'the divel in such a likenesse'.

This chapter commences by simply asserting that Fleming invented the Black Dog story. But the truth may not be so simple. It has already been pointed out that he could be discredited for reporting that deaths took place in the Bungay nave, and many would therefore have disbelieved the Black Dog element as well. But who, or what, was responsible was a matter of belief. It is perfectly possible that in a superstitious age terrified parishioners facing death could believe in, or mentally 'see' a Satanic protagonist in the form of a Black Dog. This belief may have been reported to him. There was no point in adding in such a sensational phenomenon if it would only be dismissed as nonsense, discrediting him as a reliable reporter. He must have thought it likely that it would be believed by his readers, and it seems likely that he must in some way have believed in it himself. Although he had a vested interest in making his tract as scintillating as possible to attract a wide readership, what he wrote must remain true to what he had heard, be acceptable to himself as a Christian, and convincing enough to escape widespread criticism and contradiction. We have no reason to doubt that he was sincere, and reported what he had heard in a sincere spirit. It would not be surprising if he embellished some of the details in a way which might not be factual but would add lustre to his main message, that sinful mankind must heed God's warnings, and concentrate on seeking forgiveness and living virtuous lives. But this is not the same thing as asserting that he entirely invented the Black Dog subject matter.

Fleming seems to have believed that such manifestations of evil spirits could appear, and there were precedents, as David has mentioned in Chapter 1, in relation to the dog phenomenon in Trier Cathedral in 896, and the account by John Stow of 'a thing of ugly shape and sight' in St. Michael's Church, Cornhill, London, in 1538, that is still within living memory for many people in 1577. Thunderstorms were not considered to be natural occurrences caused by warm currents of air hitting cold currents, as we know today, but the effect of God or some other supernatural power intervening in the atmosphere to create frightening and sometimes fateful incidents. There was a belief at the time, that not only could thunderstorms be averted by the ringing of the church bells, but also that if you collected consecrated water from the church font or holy water stoups and sprinkled it on your house it would not be struck by lightning. In other words, that magical powers associated with the Christian priesthood, could protect against evil forces in the universe.

It can also be suggested that even though Fleming had not accurately reported some of the facts (and this may have been due to misinformation reported to him) and even if there was controversy in the town about whether a black dog had been seen or not, many superstitious people might automatically believe Fleming's story. Firstly, because it was entirely credible to the mind-frame of the pre-modern age, and, as already mentioned, it had happened elsewhere. And secondly, because Fleming was an educated man, a man who had studied at university, a man who might become, and did in fact become an ordained priest. In a period when the majority of men and women could neither read nor write, anyone with extensive education and knowledge was viewed with a degree of respect bordering on veneration. So, if Fleming said there was a black dog, well, yes – there was a black dog, only ordinary peasant class people in Bungay were not perhaps clever enough to have actually seen it. The Church authorities in the town, the Vicar and Churchwardens might deny it but they could be wrong: and this view relates to the turmoil still occurring in parish communities following the Reformation upheavals. In fact, the local Church authorities in the town were already mistrusted, because it was they who had robbed the churches not only of the imagery and furniture donated or bequeathed by local families, and often of great personal significance for the community, but had also stripped out, destroyed, or sold, many of the features which could provide a magic protection for local people. They were the very ones who had paved the way for the Black Dog to penetrate into the town's holiest place and who could tell what worse events might follow? Why should ordinary working-class people not believe this clever writer from the great city of London, who had perhaps, it seemed, pointed out the whole truth of the matter? [23]

So deciding on the authenticity of Fleming's account from a viewpoint of nearly 450 years later, is no easy matter. In the next chapter, a look at the state of religion, society, and belief, in Bungay in the latter part of the sixteenth century may help in establishing a context for what was involved. But in relation to the important factor of the 'eye-witnesses', it is worth perhaps just drawing attention to a particular section of the community who might have been Fleming's informants. The St. Mary's parishioners worshipping in the church on that Sunday morning, may not have seen a Black Dog and may have denied that one was responsible for the tragedy. After all, they would not wish to be identified as sinners, and singled out for punishment, nor laughed at and jeered by the riff-raff of the parish, so had good reason to keep the episode hushed up. The vicar, in particular,

---

23   The context of Reformation belief and social turmoil in Bungay will be discussed
       in the next chapter.

may have preferred to remain tight-lipped. But members of Holy Trinity, the other main parish church in the town, could take a mischievous delight in pointing the finger of derision. Being a town with the unusual characteristic of having two parish churches close together, competition and rivalry between them may have been common and perhaps formed a familiar part of Bungay life in the Tudor period.

As with all organizations in the same line of business there is often rivalry, sometimes friendly, sometimes not, and sometimes envy and enmity, quarrels, conflict and even deliberate acts of revenge. The parishes of St. Mary's and Holy Trinity were not immune from this type of discord. The two churches stand within a short distrance of each other within the town centre. Holy Trinity is the older of the two buildings, with a Saxon tower perhaps used as a look-out point against Danish invasion in earlier times. It must be one of the five churches mentioned in the Domesday Book national survey of 1086, and is now considered as one of Bungay's oldest and most precious buildings. St. Mary's was the Priory Church attached to the twelfth century Priory for Benedictine nuns. The Priory was wealthy, attracting a great many grants of money and gifts of land. Money was also donated for the building of the priory church in the fourteenth century, with additions and improvements continuing until the late fifteenth century. Local wills of the period include bequests for the building of the lofty tower, completed in about 1480, and a landmark for many miles around. Raised to the greater glory of God, it was also a symbol of the prestige of the Benedictine community, patronized by many of the aristocracy and landed gentry of the region.

Holy Trinity, on the other hand never attracted such generosity. The church is considerably smaller and with its stumpy Saxon tower, is rather dwarfed by the lofty and elegant structure of St. Mary's. It clearly had a shortage of income, because the chancel had fallen into ruin by 1558, and was not finally rebuilt until 1926.[24] The historian, Dr. J. J. Raven, writing in the mid-Victorian period, remarked that, 'There is little in the poor Perpendicular architecture of the Church which calls for special notice.' [25]

On the other hand, St. Mary's church is described as:

---

24   Mann, E. *Old Bungay.* 94.

25   Mann, E. *Old Bungay.* 89.

A large and handsome structure, the north aisle being of great architectural beauty and the tower finely ornamented. Situated in the centre of the town, this imposing edifice contributes very materially to the importance of its appearance, and when the open Market Place extended from the present churchyard to the head of Bridge Street the church and convent must have presented a striking prospect to the traveller approaching Bungay from the west and north.[26]

The Priory Church did, and still does indeed dominate the centre of the town. The Priory had extensive lands running from the market place as far as the Olland Street gates at the south end of the main street, as well as other land stretching downhill to the River Waveney which divides Bungay in Suffolk from Ditchingham in Norfolk. Holy Trinity however, stands in a much less conspicuous position, in a side street, to the rear of St. Mary's. Entering the town centre, then and now, you would hardly notice its presence.

Apart from some jealousy relating to their difference in status, there may also have been some resentment concerning the church bells. St. Mary's Church has a full peal of eight bells – it is not quite clear whether there were eight in the Tudor period, but there seems to have been at least six. Holy Trinity, on the other hand, only has one bell, a tolling bell, which, in the sixteenth century, was hung, not in the church tower, but in a cage in the churchyard. There are numerous details relating to its erection in the Trinity Churchwardens' Accounts in 1566. In this respect Trinity parishioners must have felt inferior, and perhaps envied their more affluent and better-endowed neighbour. One wonders how they must have felt when they learned that the St. Mary's belfry had been badly damaged in the thunderstorm of 1577, and that the two bell-ringers had been killed; and this only a few years after their own single new bell had been installed at considerable expense.

Thus the closeness of the two buildings, which for many centuries virtually shared the same churchyard, and the difference in their size and importance, may often have been a cause of friction. In 1514 a serious dispute broke out between the two parishes. It was the custom on Corpus Christi day, a special church festival and feast day, for the parishioners to parade their banners in procession around the town. The town bailiff at this time was Richard Wharton, who acted on behalf of Thomas Howard,

---

26   Mann, E. *Old Bungay.* 37.

2nd Duke of Norfolk, the lord of the manor, and owner of Bungay Castle. Holy Trinity Church members protested that on this occasion, Wharton, with four companions: 'At eleven of the clock, on the Friday at night next after Corpus Christi day, did break down five pageants (banners) of the said inhabitants (of Holy Trinity parish), that is to say, Heaven Pageant, Pageant of All the World, Paradise Pageant, Bethlehem Pageant, and Hell Pageant; the which were ever wont to be carried about the said town upon the said day in honour of the Blessed Sacrament.' The banners were probably made of costly fabric embroidered with coloured silks and gilt threads, and highly prized by the church officials.

The occurrence was so serious that it was taken for appeal to the court of Star Chamber, the King's Council, which met in the palace of Westminster in London. Wharton protested his innocence claiming that the accusations made against him were 'untrue, feigned and imagined' and that he had met his accusers 'over a pottel of ale', supplied by him, and had agreed to assist in the restoration of the pageants. It is not known how the dispute was resolved, but it seems likely that with the support and protection of his noble lord, Wharton won the day. The Duke was the patron of St. Mary's parish, whereas the benefice of Holy Trinity was outside his sphere of interest, being appropriated to the Abbey of Barlings in Lincolnshire. In addition, Thomas Woodcock, one of Wharton's allies in the attack on the pageants, was a churchwarden of St. Mary's. So although few details are known, it seems that the attack was occasioned by a degree of enmity between the opposing parish representatives, creating controversy throughout the town, and ill-feeling which would continue to reverberate long after the court case had been dealt with at the Star Chamber. Some would support the stance of Richard Wharton (who continued in office as Town Bailiff for several years later), and some the offended sufferers of Holy Trinity.[27]

What is not clear is to what extent there may have been ongoing religious differences between the two parishes, which would exacerbate any social rivalry between the parish communities in the later Reformation period. It is certainly possible that Holy Trinity adopted a more Protestant stance during the Reformation, and that St. Mary's may have adopted a more conservative attitude preferring to retain some of the vestiges of the early pre- Reformation liturgy and church furnishings. The fact that senior church representatives of St. Mary's had objected to their church

---

27   Frank Grace, 'The Battle of Bungay', 1514–1518, *Suffolk Review*, Vol. 5, No.1, Summer, 1980. Published by the Suffolk Local History Council, Ipswich.

wardens taking down the screen between the Chancel and the nave (which will be discussed in more detail in the next chapter), may have been viewed with disapproval by Holy Trinity parishioners, and it is interesting that this dispute which caused trouble amongst St. Mary's own congregation, occurred in the April of 1577, i.e. only about three months before the disastrous thunderstorm. The conflict amongst their own members could be pointed to by Trinity representatives as a reason why the Black Dog, or 'the Devil in such a likeness', had arrived in the church to wreak revenge: and many other people in the town might have believed this version of the event.

What can be affirmed is that the townspeople would ask why St. Mary's had been targeted by the thunderstorm, when the nearby church of Holy Trinity was unscathed. In a superstitious age, when all troubles and disasters were interpreted as God's punishment for sin, they could come to only one conclusion. They deserved it. Some self-righteous members of Holy Trinity might adopt a 'Holier than Thou' attitude, and delight in mischief-making by spreading the story as far afield as possible to make fun of their snooty and affluent neighbours. Similarly, the Roman Catholics would have good reason to point the finger of derision at the St. Mary's congregation, but, as a small and persecuted minority in the Elizabethan period, nobody would have believed them. A century later, they were suspected of causing the Great Fire which virtually demolished the town.

So in summation, it is quite likely that this was the version of the event which may have reached Abraham Fleming's ears, and caused him to write his pamphlet in the way he did. His informers may have claimed to have heard the story from eyewitnesses not be eye-witnesses and Fleming would be delighted at the opportunity to relate an episode which not only concurred with his own views as to how Satan in various diabolic guises can be directly involved with punishment, but also with his life's main purpose – urging mankind to repent in order to enter into the Kingdom of Heaven and enjoy Eternal Life hereafter.

It is also interesting to note that during its subsequent history, St. Mary's Church was severely damaged by the Great Fire of 1688, whereas Holy Trinity was virtually untouched, and that in 1978 it was St. Mary's which was declared redundant by the church authorities and ceased to be fully functional as a place of worship, leaving Trinity as the sole Anglican benefice. Both these events would have been deemed evidence of God's displeasure with St. Mary's parishioners, had they occurred in the more superstitious Tudor period.

The question asked at the beginning of this chapter – *Why has Fleming's Black Dog story continued to capture the popular imagination, and what significance did it have for local people at the time of the event,* has not yet been answered. In the following chapter, an investigation of the social and religious context in Bungay in the late sixteenth century, will provide part of the answer, and may also reveal reasons why the story captures the imagination, and stimulates controversy to this very day.

It is a story which continues to make the little town of Bungay and Blythburgh popular tourist resorts for the many visitors who come every year, intent on discovering 'where it all happened'.

2

Life and Times in Elizabethan Bungay

On the last day of April 1577 John Mannock and Edward Ffylld, Churchreeves, were by the commandment of the Right Rev. Father in God, Edmund, Lord Bishop of Norwich discharged from their office for breaking down and spoiling the partition between the chancel and the church, contrary to the Queen her Majesties laws and the assent of the parishioners.[28]

In the introductory chapter, David refers to the reactions of two children, on hearing the story about the Black Dog. The narrative they were told is the one contained in Abraham Fleming's pamphlet. Each child believed the story to be true, and reacted in different ways. It's clear that both were deeply frightened, Charlotte becoming so distressed that she was in tears, and David's daughter anxious to believe that the Dog was dead, because she had found one of its claws. In other words, if he was dead, she had no reason to feel terrified that he might attack humans again.

A few years ago, I was asked to give a talk about the Black Dog to Bungay Primary School pupils. The subject is on their curriculum because it forms a significant part of local history. The children, about forty of them, were about six - to nine-years-old, and they assembled with their teachers and some parents in St. Mary's Church where the historic event had occurred. I narrated the story, and then because they seemed very concerned about it, emphasized that the event had happened a long time ago, and there was no reason to fear that the Black Dog might still be around.

At this point, one girl shot up her hand, and said, 'Please Sir, he is still alive. My Granny's seen him!' Other children then made similar comments. It was impossible to deny their claims, and so many others amongst them must have returned home believing that the fierce phantom hound that

---

28   Inscription cited from, Lummis, W. M. *The Churches of Bungay*. British Publishing Company Ltd: Gloucester, 1950. 12.

could kill, was still alive and well and living in Bungay. The following week, the history teacher who had arranged the visit, phoned to tell me that he had received several complaints from parents. Their children were so disturbed by the story, that they had been crying or having nightmares. The teacher and I were surprised at this reaction. I had been careful to word my account as gently as possible, and it seemed strange that children, who are now regularly fed a diet of extremely horrifying events on TV and videos, should respond so alarmingly to an old folk tale.

These anecdotes help towards providing an answer to the questions posed in the preceding chapter. The Black Dog narrative engenders a response at a primitive level of understanding, typical of children before they gain knowledge and acquire a more rational comprehension of human life. At the same time, it can be argued that all humans are born with an innate terror of being savaged and eaten by beasts, because we are part of the evolutionary chain of development from animal to man, involving hunting and being hunted, from the beginning of life on earth. These instincts and fears remain deep inside us, never to be eradicated. They can be detected in children at play in activities of being chased and caught. They love games, such as 'What's the time, Mr. Wolf', in which the character chosen as the Wolf chases after the rest to catch them and gobble them up for his supper. But their delight is also tinged with an innate terror of attack and capture, which adds an extra frisson of excitement to their play.

Adults obviously view the Black Dog story with less concern, but it continues to fascinate them. Many people continue to affirm that they have encountered phantom black dogs such as the East Anglian Black Shuck, and have been hair-raisingly terrified. Sometimes, it's claimed they have suffered personal tragedies, accidents, disasters, or the death of a loved one, as a result of the encounter. Some, it seems, have even died as a result. Unless they possessed a mental pre-disposition to fear such encounters, it can be argued that they could not have occurred. It might also be argued that the Bungay parents who reacted so strongly to the story being told to their children did so, because they themselves found it innately disturbing, in fact, more so than many of the horror programmes they permit their children to watch on TV.

And like their children, they may also retain some degree of fear that phantom dogs might still be around, not just creatures that belong to the historic past, or live only inside television or story books.

So the Black Dog event, even though it occurred nearly 450 years ago, continues to have the power to shock. Fleming, it seems, tapped a raw nerve in the universal human mind — the innate fear of being attacked and killed by a wild beast, all the more horrible because this beast unlike the one that attacked David's cat, can never be captured or exterminated, but continues to roam throughout time seeking for its next victims.

The anecdotes quoted, referring to children, are particularly appropriate, because the adult mind in the mediaeval and Tudor period was similarly childlike in its understanding of the natural world and how it operates. They were living in the pre-scientific age, and were ignorant of much that we take for granted today, and which helps us to cope with everyday life in a rational manner. In particular, their world was God-centred, and not on the

Black Dog pictures, 2004, Courtesy of Bungay Primary School.

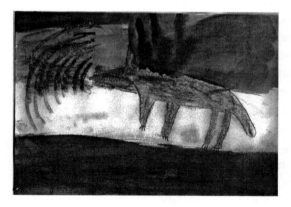

loving and caring God that Christianity preaches today, but on a God who was prepared to punish sins, both in this world, and with future torments in Purgatory and Hell. During Queen Elizabeth's reign, the Ten Commandments were displayed on the walls of every parish church in the country, to remind the congregation of their duties. Disobeying them was terrifyingly banged into their heads every Sunday by 'hellfire and damnation' Protestant clergy such as Abraham Fleming. Only about a quarter of the population could read and write, many people were engaged in boring and repetitive jobs which did not exercise or expand their minds, and ignorance was rife, particularly amongst the poor who comprised the largest section of society. In addition, the rural towns and parishes were cut off from direct communication with the wider world, and news and new ideas were slow to reach them. So it's hardly surprising if catastrophic events such as that of 1577 affected them with the same degree of shock and fear that children might feel in similar circumstances today, lacking the understanding to assess and come to terms with such a horrifying situation.

It is also worth noting the extent to which overt supernaturalism permeated the culture of early modern England. As Emma Wilby comments in her analysis of the folklore surrounding the Witch crazes of East Anglia nearly a century later, the physically demanding and harsh world of Reformation era England was also profoundly enchanted in the popular mind and this left a deeply entrenched legacy of rich folklore that continues to this day as we will discuss in the next chapter. It is hard for the modern western mind living in relative luxury and physical ease and a world dominated by science to conceive of a world view where prayers are answered, spirits can cause blessing and misfortune and the devil seems a real and apparent danger to life and limb. Whilst the hard work and skill of the people helped them deal with the demands of a life much harsher than our own they also had to contend with a spiritual world which seemed as ominous and real to them as the weather and planting crops.[29]

They had good reason to be horrified. They were already in a state of alarm and confusion, suffering from the effects of the English Reformation, arguably the most traumatic period in the country's entire history. During a period of about twenty years, that is, just one generation, the greater part of the population had seen the beliefs which they had held since infancy, shattered. The Holy Catholic Church, which comprised the only true faith for the whole of mediaeval Europe, with its centuries of tradition and religious beliefs, had been condemned by their own king, Henry VIII and some of his high-ranking clergy, and was no longer to be tolerated. It was to be replaced with a new Church of England with the king himself as its head. It was even more shocking than Charles Darwin's revelations of the origin

29   Wilby, E. Cunning *Folk and Familiar Spirits: Shamanic Traditions in Early Modern British Witchcraft and Magic*. Sussex Academic Press: Brighton. 2005. 9–10.

of species for God-fearing Victorians in the nineteenth century. In fact, it could be argued that the impact was considerably more profound, because the refutation of the papacy was accompanied by a radical shake-up of every aspect of traditional church and parish life.

In the experience of the people of Bungay, the conflict between church and state and thence Puritanism and Catholicism had been developing for some time. In 1514, for example, (as noted in the previous chapter) on Corpus Christi day, the Pageants of the guild of Holy Trinity were paraded around the town displaying images of 'hevyn', 'the pageant of all the world', 'paradys', 'Bethlehem' and 'Helle.' Later that evening at eleven o'clock the pageants were attacked, broken and thrown down by a group of townsmen led by Richard Wharton, bailiff of the Duke of Norfolk. Whilst the group refused to confess and agreed to have the pageants restored at their own expense it seems likely that Wharton and his followers were motivated by a deeply set antagonism against rituals they perceived to represent the corruption of the church hierarchy. This seems later confirmed by Wharton's zeal during his service with Thomas Cromwell when he was actively engaged in the suppression of the monasteries.[30] Similar disturbances were recorded in 1537 and given the Duke of Norfolk's position as patron of St. Mary's Church and his bailiff's noted antagonism towards the other main church of the town centre this conflict must have been a source of conflict and anxiety amongst the towns people.

However, few would have expected the level to which reformist conflict with the Catholic Church would reach. Perhaps the first signs of the coming transformation as far as the people of Bungay were concerned came with the Dissolution of the Monasteries in 1536, when all religious houses, monasteries and priories were closed, the monks and nuns dispersed and the buildings, their possessions and lands, seized for the benefit of the royal coffers. It continued during the reign of the young Edward VI with profound changes in liturgy, and a complete transformation of the church interiors. What was most bewildering for ordinary people, was that whereas in the past, the acceptance of the Catholic Church and its traditions was universally respected (even if grumbled about), and everybody knew where they stood in relation to God and the church, now not even the monarchs and clergy could agree as to what was right. Edward's radical programme of Protestant reform commenced in 1547, was soon demolished by Mary

---

30   MacCulloch, D. *Suffolk and the Tudors: Politics and Religion in an English County.* Prentice Hall: London. 1986.

Tudor who reinstated traditional Catholic forms of worship and belief only six years later, and savagely punished by burning, those who continued to support his views. Then, when Mary died and was succeeded by Elizabeth I, all changed again, much of the Edwardian Protestantism was revived, but confusingly some traditional Catholic elements were retained, while those who continued to wholeheartedly support the Roman Catholic faith were persecuted in turn.

Reading about this in history books, and with the value of hindsight, makes it all seem so simple and indeed inevitable. But it could not have felt at all like that for ordinary parishioners, such as those in Bungay, who remained shocked and perplexed, robbed of old beliefs and certainties and nothing to offer new hope or security. For, with religion in such a state of

Holy Trinity Church, Bungay

turmoil, in a few years time it could all change again under a new regime. As Edward Crouzet comments in his history of the Catholic Church in Bungay, the loss of the traditional mass and the veneration of Mary and the Saints, believed to be able to intercede for the Christian faithful on earth would have been a traumatic experience. Similarly, the Chapel of St. Thomas Beckett was placed under a general ban in 1538 and defaced the following year. Henry VIII decanonized the Saint and ordered the destruction of all memorials to him and the popular association of St. Thomas Beckett with opposition to Royal encroachment on the rights of the church made it a natural target.[31] The Chapel itself was associated closely with the Benedictine Priory attached to St. Mary's, and the ruins of the priory can still be seen to this day in the rear of the churchyard. The chapel itself was perhaps also dissolved in the same year. The importance of monastic life as the centre of moral, spiritual and intellectual power combined with the Benedictine Priory's contribution to the fabric of town life through charities, employment, education and care for the destitute and ill would have had a substantive destabilizing impact on town life.[32]

As in most parishes, the Tudor records about the changes that had occurred in Bungay are scanty. What people actually felt is largely unrecorded and can only be deduced from items noted in the church accounts. To what extent the townspeople felt loyalty to traditional Catholic beliefs and forms of worship or welcomed Protestant reforms is difficult to assess. There must have been much diversity of opinion, some with extreme views on either side, but the majority perhaps remained in favour of the old religion because of a natural conservatism and the social disruption caused by the collapse of traditional social life and values brought on by the Reformation. Roy Robinson, in his book on the history of Bungay's independent church now known as Emmanuel, comments that whilst there seemed to be a nominal agreement as to the need for a unified national Church, amongst the Bungay townsfolk there was a diverse range of opinions as to the form that should take. Many seemed content with orthodox Episcopal rule; others wanted to move towards a Scottish styled Presbyterian system and still more wanted to have religious freedom to pursue their own religious beliefs as conscience dictated. It was these latter groups who first split from the Anglican Church to form their own independent and non-conformist chapels.[33]

However, some probably harboured a long-standing desire for reform. In the late fourteenth century, the Waveney Valley region was identified as expressing support for the teachings of John Wycliffe (c. 1330-84). An Oxford radical philosopher, he questioned both papal authority and the clergy's right to property, and argued that rather than the tenets of the Church, the word of God as revealed in the Bible was the only sure source of authority in religion. His views were condemned as subversive by Pope

---

31 Crouzet E. *Slender Thread: The Origins and History of the Benedictine Mission in Bungay 1657–2007.* Downside Abbey Books: Bath, 2007. 2–3.

32 Reeve, C. *Straunge and Terrible Wunder.* 8.

33 Robinson, R. *God's People in Bungay and Denton: The Story of Bungay's Independent Church,* Later to be Called the Congregational Church (United Reformed & Methodist). 3.

Gregory XI, and he and his followers, who became known as Lollards, were expelled from Oxford. An important result of his teachings was that the first English translation of the Bible was published in the 1390s. After his death his views remained popular in some quarters and Foxe's *Book of Martyrs* records that 120 men in the Waveney area were tried and convicted of anti-papal views between 1428 and 1431. These included six from Beccles, one from Shipmeadow, and one from Bungay, but there must have been many more who were interested or sympathetic but dare not commit themselves to open support for fear of the consequences which were ultimately terrifying: death by burning. Of those convicted, most recanted and were allowed to go free after suffering public whippings in the market place, but their leader, William White was burnt at the stake in Norwich in 1428.[34]

Such severe punishments for profoundly felt Christian beliefs must have elicited a certain degree of sympathy from the local community. Those who had been punished would continue to retain their beliefs, even if they could no longer openly express them, and they, their family and friends would continue to hope and pray for the day when some reformer might appear with the power to create a Christian Church more in keeping with the simple tenets of the Gospels. Keeping this faith alive became a focus of their Christian commitments. So when, in the early part of the sixteenth century, information spread regarding a new zeal for reform in Europe connected with the name of Martin Luther in Germany, they must have thought that at last their prayers were being answered. Quite what they thought about Henry VIII's denouncement of the Pope in Rome is another matter. From a Christian point of view his motives were hardly virtuous, for his aim was chiefly to obtain a divorce from his wife, and retain a greater amount of money for his own expenditure instead of paying it into the Catholic coffers. Nevertheless it was a beginning which might lead to better things, and they would be considerably cheered by other reforms during the Henrician era, notably the Dissolution of the Monasteries, and the plans to use some of the income derived from the sale of buildings and land to create grammar schools for the education of the young.

The edicts condemning superstitious practices must also have been welcomed, and Henry's authorization of an English Bible. Then, when Edward VI came to the throne, and introduced a widespread reform on the lines of developments in other parts of Europe, success, it seemed,

---

34   Page, W. *Victoria County History of Suffolk*. Vol. 2. 1907.

was finally assured.

Those with a burning zeal for reform however, were in a minority but typically better educated, more articulate than the majority of their fellow townsfolk. Although there might be widespread support for some of the changes in religion, the new simple emphasis on the Word of God as expressed in the Scriptures meant little to those parishioners who had highly valued the ritual, pageantry, and supernatural aspects of Roman Catholicism. Their lives tended to be hard: they commenced manual labour from an early age, suffered a great deal from ill-health caused by poor diet and ineffective forms of medicine, women frequently died in childbirth, many children died in infancy, disease was rife and they often lived at subsistence level particularly during the winter when food was in short supply. What the Catholic religion had offered was a comforting belief in the magical transformation of their lives achieved through the support of the clergy, the Saints in heaven, and the Holy Family, helping them cope with the deprivations that poverty inflicted on both mind and body.

Wall hanging in St. Mary's Church, depicting the Black Dog (centre).
It was designed and made by Mary Walker with a team of local embroiderers.

The Catholic Church with its emphasis on the intercession of the saints and the comforting maternal role of the Virgin Mary, the richness of its church interiors with so much decoration and colour to delight the eye, its rituals, candles and processions creating a sort of vision of heaven on earth, continues to offer similar support for impoverished communities throughout the world today. But in the mediaeval and early modern periods its impact was much greater because superstition was more widespread even amongst educated sections of the community. The Holy Family and the saints in heaven were invested with the absolute power of achieving miracles, alleviating poverty, curing sickness, comforting the bereaved, and offering an eternal life of bliss in Heaven, for those who worshipped in the Catholic faith. The parishioners presented them with gifts, prayed devoutly to them both inside and outside the church, and begged them for support in their needs and sufferings. They believed that everything connected with the church was holy. They would steal consecrated water from the font or holy-water stoups by the entrance doors, and communion bread, crediting them with magical powers that could help in all sorts of ways, such as curing sickness in humans and beasts, or averting the entry of evil spirits or damage by thunderstorms to their houses. Scraps of paper with the words of the Lord's Prayer written upon them were also a magical omen, and, if you uttered the words of the prayer or other holy creeds, further dangers could be vanquished. The great painted image of St. Christopher which faced the entrance door in St. Mary's, could act as a protection if you supplicated before it on first entering the church. It provided a safeguard for travellers, but also against sudden death, the worst fate for mediaeval Christians as it was believed that unless you received absolution from your sins by a priest, you could not enter Heaven but would be condemned to Purgatory, or worse, might roast in Hell throughout all Eternity.

This summary provides some idea of the early modern cast of mind, and the extent to which Roman Catholicism, the priesthood and the richly decorated church interiors, catered for the needs of the people. Imagine then, the shock and horror of the parishioners when, during the reign of Edward VI, the church authorities and local churchwardens commenced a rigorous programme of stripping the churches bare. It wasn't just that church furnishings such as the altars, pews, and rood-lofts containing images of Christ on the Cross, supported by Saints Mary and John, were removed, but that many other venerated interior features were sold, smashed up, or carried out to be burnt on bonfires. The ancient and colourful wall-paintings depicting Saints, Biblical stories, or images such as the Last Judgement, which for generations had provided picture-book images for congregations which were mainly illiterate were now erased, scraped off or covered over with lime-wash. Carvings, paintings, and embroideries of the Holy Family and Saints were taken down, and its not clear exactly what happened to them. Some may have been sold, some may have been preserved for safe-keeping in their own homes by those clergy or church wardens who were unhappy about their removal, but many others were probably destroyed by zealous Protestants in the parish who were keen to rid their church of idolatrous Popish trumpery once and for all. Even the wonderful pictorial stained glass was scraped and the stories obliterated, or smashed to be replaced with plain glass.

Imagine the horror congregations would feel if this happened by Government edict in our churches today. It wasn't just the veneration with which these objects and images were regarded, or their supposed magical properties, nor that they provided something beautiful or interesting to gaze upon during the long tedious Latin church services. It was that they also had personal associations for some of the congregation, because they had been given, or made, or purchased to commemorate their ancestors, other relatives or friends. It's true that such gifts were usually from the wealthier members of society, but even the 'middling sort of folk' would scrimp and save to provide 'treasures' for display in the church by which they would be remembered.

Now, all these objects too, were treated literally as rubbish. They had Catholic or superstitious associations and must be destroyed. Over a period of months, gradually lengthening into years, each time the parishioners entered their church, they saw it becoming more and more empty, colourless and cheerless, as more furnishings and decorations disappeared. The little church of St. Lawrence Ilketshall, near Bungay is a good example of how the interior of the Bungay churches of Holy Trinity and St. Mary's must have looked, whitewashed, featureless and bare, once the Protestant zeal had taken its toll.

Gargoyles carved by mediaeval stone-masons along the north wall of St. Mary's, had been placed there to scare evil spirits from the church, for the protection of both the building and the parishioners. But what use were they, now the protective magic within the church had been dispersed? It could only be a matter of time before the Evil One entered and wreaked his revenge, either as the agent of God to punish those who were spoiling his Holy place, or simply because it was now so much easier for him. The church, from time immemorial the parish sanctuary, was no longer a safe place to be.

The state of fear and suspense in which the population remained at the commencement of Queen Elizabeth's reign is illustrated in the following:

When people asked the Suffolk minister John Carter whether they were to expect Popery again, he would reply: 'You shall not need to fear fire and faggots any more: but such dreadful divisions will be amongst God's people and professors as will equalize the greatest persecutions.' [35]

As referred to in the previous chapter, there must have been strong divisions in Bungay between reforming Protestants and traditionalist Catholics, and all the various shades of opinion in between. In particular there would be those who were shocked and disturbed by what had happened but were not sufficiently literate to express their feelings, and whose voice, even if heard, would be taken little notice of. Throughout history, the poor and uneducated have been disregarded and abused because they could not speak up for themselves, but their feelings might be as deep and their anger as vehement as those who were more eloquent.

And what they had lost was not just the solace and support the Pre-Reformation Church had to offer. They had lost much more besides. They had lost the charitable ministrations of the Benedictine nuns, who, after the closure of their Priory in 1536, were obliged to seek accommodation wherever they could find it, and may themselves have felt that the Black Dog was now howling in the midst of their former sanctuary. The nuns had provided food for the poor who gathered daily at the Priory gates, and were given the left-over morsels from their evening meal: crumbs perhaps, but crumbs that might include substantial pieces of bread, meat, fish, fruit and other delicacies which were hungrily welcomed by those living at starvation level. The nuns also provided clothing, and once a year, the Prioress gave a sum of money to be distributed for the benefit of the poor.

In addition, leisure activities, traditionally enjoyed by all sections of the townspeople, were curtailed. The Protestants disapproved of pleasure. It smacked of the Devil, and might lead to vice, and that might lead to eternal damnation. The Ale Games generally held as church fund-raising events at Whitsuntide were increasingly condemned and finally banned. They occurred after Whit Sunday, in late May or June when the weather was becoming warmer, and the evenings lighter, and the principal event was usually a theatrical performance with a Biblical theme, produced and acted by the parishioners, with nearly everybody in the community involved in one way or another. It was the sort of tradition that bound the townsfolk together in fellowship, all working towards a common aim, and each person feeling valued for what he or she had to offer. Those who couldn't act or

35 Collinson, P. *The Birthpangs of Protestant England*. Macmillan: London, 1988. 29.

Mediaeval gargoyles on the North wall of St. Mary's Church

perform music could assist with cooking or serving food, or brewing the ale, or sewing costumes, or building the stage and scenery. All shared in the feasting at the end of the event, which took place in either the church-yards, or in the Castle Yard, which was a traditional area for recreation once the Bigod family who owned the property had vacated it in the fourteenth century.

The Puritans argued that these events resulted in drunkenness and debauchery. However, in the view of many of the parishioners, little real harm was done, everybody had enjoyed themselves, the church had gained much needed funds, and the event was very much the highlight of the social year, as important in its own way as Christmas or Easter. But Ale Games were increasingly condemned and finally banned. They survived until 1591, fourteen years after the Black Dog event, but Puritan disapproval was another element creating increasing friction by 1577, and causing the new style religion they represented to become, amongst some sections of the community, deeply resented.

Furthermore, in the context of the defeat of the Spanish Armada in 1558 and the intensity of antagonism felt for the secular government by many remaining Catholics (perhaps most famously illustrated by the Gunpowder Plot by Guy Fawkes in 1605) support for artwork, rituals and festivals perceived to have Catholic influences was not just heretical but potentially treasonous. Churches which engaged in traditional rituals and related festivities were potentially guilty of an underhanded reintroduction of Catholicism which could not only undermine the gains made by Puritans towards their ideal of a simpler and purer faith but also undermine the legitimacy and authority of the crown.[36]

Puritans also disapproved of any work or entertainments on a Sunday, which should be strictly set aside for focusing upon God alone: as the Commandments, now prominently displayed in every church interior proclaimed: 'Remember the Sabbath Day and keep it Holy'. That was all very well, but for ordinary folk, Sunday was the only day of the week when they didn't have to work. They felt that if they attended the church service in the morning and paid their respects to their Saviour, surely they might be allowed to spend the remainder of the day as they pleased. Puritans condemned trading, which meant that shops and ale-houses should be closed, there must be no games, dancing or sports, and even travel unless it was essential, should be restricted. They would prefer that their parishioners spent the day reading the Bible or books of sermons (although the majority still couldn't read) and attending both morning and evening services, or otherwise occupy themselves in seemly tasks, holy conversation, and reflection.

So not just the church, but social life too, was affected by the new regime of Godliness and, from a contemporary perspective, gloominess. In the 1570s, Puritanism was just developing and was not as strict as it was to become in the early seventeenth century, especially during the Cromwellian era, when even the celebrations surrounding Christmas were temporarily banned. But it was becoming more pronounced, so even if certain Sunday pleasures were still permitted, the general air of disapproval from the leading churchmen must have daunted the enthusiasm of those who only wanted a bit of time to relax and have fun on their only free day. That old phrase about 'having the *black dog* on your back', referring to depression or misery, might here be deemed appropriate for the sort of mood the Puritans were inflicting upon those who didn't share their solemn views concerning religious observance.

In the years leading up to 1577, internal divisions were becoming more pronounced within St. Mary's Church. They were partly affected by national events. Edmund Grindal replaced Mathew Parker as Archbishop

---

36   Robinson, R. *God's People in Bungay and Denton*. 3.

of Canterbury in 1575. He was more Puritanical in spirit than his predecessor, and his views did not please the pleasure-loving Queen Elizabeth. The dichotomy between those who favoured the retention of some aspects of Catholicism, such as the Queen herself, and those who, like Grindal favoured a Puritanical extreme, continued to create tension and conflict. It seemed that, in the words of John Strype in his Annals of the Reformation (and also quoted in Painting-Stubbs as above) the whole country had been corrupted by the Devil, by 'wolves and foxes' who crept out in the absence of 'good shepherds'.[37]

In Bungay, a violent clash of opinions resulted in further conflict and controversy. On April 30, 1577, two church reeves of St. Mary's were accused of destroying the rood-screen that stood between the chancel and the nave. They were John Mannock and Edward Ffylld.[38] The rood-screen divided the chancel, the sacred area reserved for the priests at the east end of the church, from the nave which is where the congregation sat or stood for church services. The mediaeval wooden screens were usually elaborately carved and brightly coloured with painted images of saints. They were a striking and prominent feature of church interiors, much venerated by parishioners, because they could personally relate to the saints depicted. The rood-loft above was occupied by a large carving of Christ on the Cross, flanked by the two saints who had supported him after his crucifixion, Mary and John, and these images in such a prominent position would also be familiar and dear to the congregation. Diarmid MacCulloch has commented :

> The furniture of the rood and its screen was one of the most prominent features of the mediaeval church, and with its symbolic position separating the priest's chancel from the people's nave, the screen was a natural focus for Reformation conflicts which might split a village. [39]

The churchwardens' accounts had already recorded that Edward Molle, the church carpenter, had been paid to remove the rood-screen and carved images during the reign of Edward. He later restored them during the reign of Mary, and then removed them again when Elizabeth ascended the throne. It would seem, however, that although he had removed the carved figures

---

37   O.U.P. Clarendon Press, 1826, Vol 11. Part 11. 145.

38   Lowestoft Record Office 1116/E1/1, f. 162.

39   MacCulloch, D. *Suffolk and the Tudors.*

from the rood-loft he had not been asked to take down the rood-screen. Now, the church reeves took the matter into their own hands, and removed it themselves. They certainly took no care in performing the task, ripping it out in great haste, anxious to get the job done before they were detected and prevented: for the words used in the citation against them were 'breaking down and spoiling' it. It was also stated in the Bishop's citation that they had flagrantly disobeyed 'a commandment before sent unto them' by the parish priest and churchwardens. Church reeves seem to have been a lesser sort of church dignitary with their own particular responsibilities.

One of the two churchwardens who held office during that year was John Edwards. He was a member of a prominent Bungay family which had been connected with St. Mary's for a number of years. In the Church-wardens' Accounts Book, he describes the partition, or screen, as 'very comely & decently made, according to the Queen her Majesty's laws': But somebody has underlined this phrase in the Register and added: 'John Edwards here Lyes, for it was full of Immagery not defaced.' [40] This must have been written, either by Mannock or Ffylld, or somebody sympathetic to their views, and was a strident comment to make, accusing a church-warden of writing lies in the church register. The entry also makes it clear that the rood-screen must have survived from Queen Mary's reign, because the imagery hadn't been 'defaced'. During Edward's reign, the screen would have been removed and probably destroyed, or had all the painted images of the Saints erased. It's not known whether it was this old screen which was re-introduced during Mary's reign, or whether a new one was made.

A further entry in the Churchwardens' Register records: 'Item: Paid to Nobbes the Sexton for making clean the church after the pulling down of the partition (rood) between the chancel & church ... contrary to a commandment before sent by the Lord Bishop of Norwich by one, John Bowbright, his man, to the inhabitants.'

So it was clear that the Puritan reforming members of the church were prepared to flout their Bishop's commandments, feeling justified in the belief that they were acting according to the spirit of the Gospels and the Reformed Church in simplifying church interiors so that the focus would be on the spoken Word of God.

Meanwhile, nationally the conflict between traditionalists and Puritans was also reaching breaking point. The Queen became further annoyed with Archbishop Grindal's Calvinist tendencies and ordered him to terminate

---

40   Lowestoft Record Office 1116/E1/1, f. 162.

the 'prophesying' meetings he was organizing, in which Puritans were encouraged to discuss matters relating to the Gospels. She saw this as subversive, and likely to lead to further conflict within church circles at a time when she felt it paramount to achieve unity after the troublesome and tortuous reign of her Catholic sister Mary. When Grindal defied her saying that he would rather offend his Queen than his God, she suspended him from office, in June 1577.

News of this event gradually reached Bungay, and added to the perplexity of the local community. With the Archbishop at odds with the Queen, and both claiming to be God's representatives for the kingdom, what were they supposed to believe? It must have further divided the town into two camps, those who supported a more traditional form of worship, and those who were keen to see all relics of Roman Catholicism abolished. The Puritans would be particularly upset at having their reforming Archbishop dismissed from office, since it augured badly for achieving their own objectives in Bungay. It seems likely that the removal of the rood-screen was a deliberate act of protest. Having been a subject of controversy since the beginning of Edward's reign in 1547, it was once again restored to its former position, presumably in about June or July of 1577. This would have caused outrage amongst those members of the congregation who believed it to have been rightly vandalised, and they may have refused to attend church services in protest. It will be remembered that when the Black Dog entered Blythburgh Church, he placed himself 'upon a main balke or beam, whereon sometime the rood did stand', and then swung down amongst the congregation and commenced his murderous assaults. Clare Painting-Stubbs has pointed out the significance of this point.[41] It would seem that in Blythburgh, the churchwardens had complied with the Bishop's commands to remove the rood and rood-screen, and the Black Dog deliberately and provocatively posed himself there in the holy place connected with Catholic devotion. However, the significance of this statement in the local context remains problematic. Was it in mockery of Roman Catholicism – Christ is now replaced by Satan? Or was it simply to make a point about the controversies the roods had been causing throughout the land? In which case it would have been more provocative if he had launched his attack from the replaced Bungay rood-screen. Perhaps on this point, Fleming had got his 'eye-witness accounts' muddled.

It has been pointed out as significant, that the Black Dog element of

41   Painting-Stubbs, C. *Religion, Familiars and Abraham Fleming.* 12.

Fleming's account is not included in the Bungay parish registers. This gives rise to the intriguing question: was it because the clerk who recorded the thunderstorm and the deaths of the two bell-ringers was either of a Catholic or Protestant persuasion, and therefore adjusted his account accordingly?

The argument in the preceding chapter has centred on whether Fleming invented the Hell-hound story for his own reasons, or whether some members of the congregation really did believe that Satan in the not unfamiliar disguise of a Black Dog was the perpetrator. But which sections of the congregation might claim this? Would it be the traditionalists because they believed the heart and soul and magical protective powers of the church had been ripped out, or the Puritans because they had been flouted in their attempt to establish a 'purer' form of worship? Either or both might have seen him, because all were in a state of confusion and alarm, a state of mind which had persisted for decades and which it seemed might never be resolved. If you cannot feel safe and at peace in your own church where then can you find peace? The Black Dog had entered as a visible symbol of all the problems and perplexities, the sufferings, imprisonments and burnings that the Reformation of religion had occasioned, finally turning a peaceful parish church into somewhere more like Hell.

3

The Black Dog of Bungay in Folklore

He takes the form of a huge black dog, and prowls along dark lanes and lonesome field footpaths, where, although his howling makes the hearer's blood run cold, his footfalls make no sound. You may know him at once, should you see him, by his fiery eye; he has but one, and that, like the Cyclops', is in the middle of his head. But such an encounter might bring you the worst of luck: it is even said that to meet him is to be warned that your death will occur before the end of the year.[42]

After the tumultuous events of 1577 there is a tremendous gap in the historical record regarding the Black Dog of Bungay. This has to do with the immense and widespread loss of historical documents and materials during the Great Fire of Bungay. The 1688 fire destroyed all but five homes and led to a substantial demographic shift in the town as destitute and homeless people fled for new opportunities elsewhere and others moved in to rebuild.[43] Another major cause of this information dearth is that there were few systemic attempts to research or catalogue the beliefs of the general population. Popular folklore, as a subject of research, had to wait until the industrial revolution to emerge in any significant way.

It was in the seventeenth century that some tantalising tales of the devil appearing in the form of a huge Black Dog or Waterhound in nearby Halesworth emerged during the Mathew Hopkins and John Stearne witch craze of the English Civil War.[44] However, despite the intriguing nature of these stories there is little to directly link them with the Black Dog of Bungay

---

42 Dutt W. A. *Highways & Byways in East Anglia.* MacMillan: London, 1901. 216.

43 Reeve, T. *The Day Bungay Burned: The Story of the great Fire of Bungay 1688.* Peter Morrow & Co: Bungay 1988. 27–30.

44 C. L'Estrange, Ewen (ed.) *Witch Hunting and Witchtrials: Indictments for Witchcraft from the records of 1373* Assisez held for the Home Circuit A.A. 1559–1736. Kegan Paul, Trench Trubner & Co: Broadway House, 1929. 294–323.

tale. They appear to be a part of the more general demonological lore which underlay the beliefs of witchcraft during the 1642-1647 panic. In a sense, this is part of the same oral tradition that gave rise to the demonic hound of Faust.[45] As previously discussed, this body of medieval and renaissance demonological folklore is most likely the origin of Abraham Fleming's retelling of the Black Dog, a re-telling which formed the basis of later inter-pretations of the 1577 legend. While there is little hard evidence of the story being in continuous oral circulation from 1577 to the present (let alone having origins dating to Pagan antiquity as some folklorists have suggested) it can be argued that there is more to the lack of evidence than simply a complete break of continuity of Black Dog folklore in Bungay.[46] Rather, we contend that due to the wide circulation of the story, the incredibly fertile ground for its revival, the enthusiasm with which it was adopted in the nineteenth and twentieth centuries and the enormous proliferation of Black Dog stories through the British Isles and the rest of Northern Europe, Black Dog legends remained part of the folklore for the entire area. This is not to maintain an argument of continuity of tradition relating specifically to the 1577 event in any linear sense, but rather to recognize that the ideas, locations, landmarks, legends and mythology were constantly evolving and developing throughout this period, in the context of an established cultural mythos which had developed since the early middle ages.

In the studies of East Anglian folklore, typified by such books as Arthur Randell's *Sixty Years a Fenman* or George Ewart Evans's *Patterns Under the Plough*, we see a continual theme of the recalcitrance of the locals to embrace modernity, their close knit communities and the importance of local folklore and superstition in everyday life held up as a bulwark against the tide of modernization, secularism and industry.[47] We find similar patterns in Ethel Mann's *Old Bungay* which extols the virtues of Bungay as a site of connectedness to the past, heritage and authentic rural culture in opposition to rootless, consumer driven modernism. This will be discussed in the next chapter. In the case of this nostalgic representation of East Anglia as a site of rural authenticity, Arthur Randell gives a very emotive description in his foreword to *Sixty Years a Fenman*,

---

45   Woods, B. A. 'The Devil in Dog Form'. 229–235; Woods, B. A. *The Devil in Dog Form*. 2–3.

46   Westwood, J. 'Friend or Foe: Norfolk Traditions of Black Shuck'. 71–72.

47   Evans, G. E. *The Pattern Under the Plough: Aspects of the Folklife of East Anglia*. Faber and Faber. 1966; Randell, A. *Sixty years a Fenman*. Routledge and Keegan Paul, 1953.

As motorways devour more and more of our countryside and villages fall victim to our modern planners, it is good that there are still countrymen who can recall and record the old scenes before they are forgotten. And not the old scenes only, but the old ways of life of the people who lived in the houses of which so many are being condemned and demolished, who worked in the fields and trudged the rough narrow roads which now lie under the broad highways along which a motorist must pass at such speed that he has no opportunity to see beyond the way ahead or to stop and wonder what was once there ...[48]

Despite its relatively close proximity to London, Cambridge and other urban cosmopolitan centres, East Anglia is culturally distinct, rural and somewhat isolated from the rest of England. However, whilst there is a legacy of multiple waves of immigration there is a high degree of shared culture which is somewhat unique in dialect, culture and folklore. East Anglia is a well defined agricultural region with its own particular geographical and cultural forms, perhaps most explicitly manifested in the fens. The impact of the witch crazes during the English Civil War has left its mark in a very pronounced legacy of folklore, customs and stories regarding witchcraft and folk remedies which were eagerly recorded by folklorists and scholars.[49] As Dr. Wollaston Groome M.D. notes in his 1895 presentation on Suffolk folklore, there is a peculiar pragmatism to Norfolk and Suffolk superstitions. The country has a history dating to the Reformation of strongly entrenched Puritanism and non-conformism (the establishment of which we have seen in the previous chapter regarding the 1577 event) and prior to that Lollardism. The region has a history of aversion to overt spectacles of ritual in superstition, instead focussing on folk remedies and beliefs barring the legacy of the witch crazes of the English Civil War. In this respect customs have tended to be intensely localized, typically personalised and kept within families and villages and are not as orientated towards the larger displays of religiosity and carnivalesque festivals as one finds, for example, in the West Country.[50] This is corroborated by Evans who defines the locals born prior to 1895 as people who 'had the lore in abundance; it was part of their existence and they had rarely paused to consider it as something separate from themselves... It was not a question of believing in

---

48   Randell, A. *Sixty Years a Fenman*. Vii.

49   Newman, L.F. 'Some Notes on the Folklore of Cambridgeshire and the Eastern Counties'. *Folklore*. Vol. 56, No. 3. September 1945. 287–293.

50   Groome, W. 'Suffolk Leechcraft'. *Transactions of the Folklore Society*. Vol. 6, No. 11, June 1895.117.

it but living it.'[51] In Evans's view, East Anglia is an area more accessible to the continent via the North Sea than to much of the rest of England and is shaped by unique agricultural habits such as the harvesting of hemp and corn. Evans argues that Norfolk and Suffolk, as a relatively isolated agricultural backwater, possess a unique culture granting insights into England's cultural heritage. As such, the study of East Anglian Folklore offers insight into 'how much of the old recently displaced culture is still alive and accessible in present society.' [52]

Bungay itself has its own array of local folklore besides that of the Black Dog myth. Dating most likely from Elizabeth Bonhote's 1796 novel, *Bungay Castle*, is the legend of the town being riddled with tunnels that connect the most prominent local historical sites such as Mettingham Castle, Bungay Castle and the Church of St. Marys. Tunnels linking the castle to the ruined priory at the back of St. Mary's Church feature prominently in Bonhote's novel and may have been inspired by the twelfth century remains of siege works found under the Castle which can still be seen today. Bonhote's novel was quite popular at the time yet was largely unknown by the end of the nineteenth century and seems to be the basis of this myth of labyrinthine tunnels. The legend is reinforced by the discovery of sealed underground chambers in the courtyard of Emmanuel Church in 1977, and many of the older buildings have cellars with archways long since sealed off. In a related myth, the Butter Cross in the centre of town is reputed to be erected on the ruins of an underground dungeon with its own network of tunnels. Another tale, perhaps dating from Bonhote or perhaps drawn from the local folklore during the eighteenth century tells the story of a white lady and a knight who haunt the ruins of Bungay Castle. The town has numerous ghost stories such as a ghostly coach pulled by four demonic steeds along the road to Geldeston often associated with the Bigods, as is the Black Dog story itself in more recent literature. Another story I was told was the belief that a local hair-dressing salon was haunted by the ghost of an elderly lady who disapproved of unmarried couples and would steal or hide objects from them whilst they were having their hair cut. A nearby relatively isolated farmstead was believed to be haunted by a young lady who became pregnant to a local landlord in the nineteenth century and as a consequence drowned herself in the pond out in front of the house. Another aspect of folklore surviving from the seventeenth century can be discerned from the numerous

---

51   Evans, George Ewart. *The Pattern Under the Plough.* 19.

52   Evans, G. E.. *The Pattern Under the Plough.* 21–22.

examples of marks and carvings in the woodwork of older buildings which acted as enchantments to protect the occupants. These tales and links to past events, beliefs and people are very common and form an integral part of local culture. Tales of the Black Dog of Bungay, people's sightings of the dog, local urban legends regarding its beats and activities and its connection with the 1577 event and evocative locations like the Castle and the Church of St. Mary all relate to this broad picture.

The Black Dog folklore is therefore set against the backdrop of a vast array of myths, ghost stories and legends and integrated together as a pan English (and for that matter pan European) mythology of the Black Dog. By 1869, in *Chamber's Book of Days*, for example, it could be said with confidence that,

> In almost every county there is a popular belief in a spectral dog, which, although slightly varying in appearance in different parts, always bears the same general characteristics. It is described as large, shaggy, and black, with long ears and tail. It does not belong to any species of living dogs, but is severally said to resemble a hound, a setter, a terrier, or a shepherd-dog, though often larger than a Newfoundland. It bears different names, but is always alike supposed to be an evil spirit, haunting places where evil deeds have been done, or where some calamity may be expected.[53]

The Victorians were the first to instigate a body of learning suggesting that the Black Dogs myths were an endemic part of the English countryside. In the 1850s, stories emerged in 'Notes and Queries', the antecedent of the ubiquitous Folklore Society, about the Shuck of Norfolk. Within a decade or so a body of study had reached the point where it could be said with some confidence that legends of ghostly, fey or demonic Black Dogs were rife throughout the British Isles with concentrations in the West Country, East Anglia and Lincolnshire–Yorkshire.[54] By the end of the nineteenth century, Black Dog legends had become synonymous with the English countryside and were seen as cultural fossils of a bygone age. The legends also served to link England (in its period of rapid and tumultuous social and industrial transformation) to antiquity with its evocative images of timelessness, stability and tradition.

There is a certain degree of mythological sleight of hand at work in these representations of Black Dog mythology. Old Shock appears in

53   Chambers, R. *The Book of Days*. Vol. 2, Philedelphia: J. B. Lippencott & co. 1869– 433.
54   Hartes, J. 'Black Dog Studies'. In Trubshaw, B. *Explore Phantom Black Dogs*. 5.

Forbys Lexicon of East Anglian vocabulary as 'a mischievous goblin, in the shape of a dog or of a calf, haunting highways and foot-paths in the dark.'[55] Similarly, other descriptions indicated that creatures, later to become Black Dogs in popular folklore, were, in the earlier part of the nineteenth century, shape-changing creatures which also appeared in the form of calves, donkeys or even large black cats.[56] By the late nineteenth and early twentieth centuries these diverse sightings had become reified into the iconic image of a huge black hound with a shaggy coat and eyes like saucers of the sort described in the 1577 Bungay event. In this evolving folklore melange there was tendency for the term Shuck to be applied to ghost stories of flesh

THE WEST VIEW OF BUNGAY CASTLE, IN THE COUNTY OF SUFFOLK.

Bungay Castle, engraved by Joshua Kirby, 1748.
This is how the Castle looked during Elizabeth Bonhote's childhood in Bungay

and blood hounds who met tragic ends. When combined with all the tales collectively placed under the banner of Black Dog folklore, the underlying narrative of a nation-wide myth of Black Dogs linked to ancestral source in antiquity seems increasingly tenuous.[57]

---

55   Forby, R. *The Vocabulary of East Anglia*. Vol. II. J. B. Nichols and Son: London. 1830 (1970). 238.

56   Hartes, J. 'Black Dog Studies.' 5–8. Reeve, C. A *Straunge and Terrible Wunder*. 71.

57   Woods, B. A. *The Devil in Dog Form*. 2–3; Theo' Brown Collection University of Exeter; Hartes, J. 'Black Dog Studies' 17.

A very important question here is raised as to why there was such fixation on Black Dog myths being fossils of a primordial past? Perhaps just as important is the question of why Folklore as a serious area of research rose from obscurity to hold such a prominent position in the national ethos? The answer to these questions lies in the unique experience of the industrial revolution in England and the unprecedented urbanization and industrialization of the late eighteenth and early nineteenth centuries. These processes (paralleled in somewhat nationally distinctive patterns in the states which were later to become Germany) formed the basis of an attempt to link the identity of the nation with the rapidly diminishing indigenous culture and landscape of the rural sector and agrarian lifestyle. Closely integrated to this approach of associating authenticity with rural culture was the perception of a static and eternal agrarian countryside into which the talented folklorist could dig for cultural fossils belonging to a primordial pagan past. By doing this one could claim to have found the cultural essence of the nation as exemplified in its cultural continuity. Driving this search was the need to redefine what national culture meant in the wake of the tumultuous changes of the industrial revolution and the massive demographic shifts of the nineteenth century.

Diarmuid O'Giollain has argued, the notion of folklore is predicated on the idea of the death of tradition. Folklore became an area of research and investigation precisely when existent rural traditions were coming under threat from industrialization, urbanization and demographic change. Tradition is closely linked with identity and has powerful emotional connections to culture and the landscape.[58] Hence the destruction of traditional ways of life and belief became a source of anxiety for people wrestling with the notion of what being English meant in the new post-industrial world. In this sense, tradition with its implications of timelessness and authority, lies at the basis of folklore and thus serves an important role in maintaining social cohesion, identity and custom. Traditions and rituals serve to define identity, to inculcate values and ideals intrinsic to community and thus work to hold society together.[59] This was particularly pertinent in an England that had not only undergone massive economic and demographic shifts during the industrial revolution but had also become the centre of a vast cosmo-

---

58 O'Giollain, D. *Locating Irish Folklore: Tradition, Modernity, Identity.* Cork University Press: Cork, 2000. 8–9.

59 Hobsbawm, E. and Ranger, T. *The Invention of Tradition.* Cambridge University Press; Cambridge, 1983. 1–5.

politan trading empire containing multiple ethnic identities, values and ways of life.

The idealization of rural England reached extraordinary levels during the late nineteenth century among folklorists, artists and historians. The level of urbanization during the post-industrial revolution era was unparalleled in history and this led to a great deal of anxiety regarding the future of English identity. There was also much concern regarding the kinds of social, environmental and physical problems these changes could create. Romantic literature and artwork of the nineteenth century was rife with contrasts between a perceived idyllic countryside linked to tradition and heritage set against a bustling, money-driven, dirty and soulless city.[60] Moreover, the rise of a large-scale urbanized population was condemned because it seemed to strip people of tradition, culture and heritage precisely at the time when these issues of identity and continuity were becoming significant in the popular imagination. These issues and romantic responses drawing on folklore, tradition and historicity were paralleled in Scotland, Wales and Ireland and much of Europe and used as a way of constructing social identity.[61]

As Ronald Hutton indicates, this new representation of rural England represents a remarkable turnaround in the literary construction of the countryside. This is particularly extraordinary given the propensity of the rural sector to be perceived as a dark place of crass manners, ignorance, superstition and brutality in contrast to urban centres which were seen as the basis of cosmopolitan enlightenment, progress, refinement and culture.[62] It is worth noting that whilst the rise of romantic representations of the countryside certainly achieved literary prominence and popularity, the alternate representation of the 'rural other' as a dark place of ignorance and superstition never disappeared. On this front, as Peter Mandler argues, the preoccupation of the rural myth was linked to specific sectors of English society and was far from a universally

---

60 For more details on these issues and representations see my earlier work Waldron, D. *The Sign of the Witch.* 72–76.

61 Waldron, D. *The Sign of the Witch.* 60-78. For those seeking more information on this topic I would also recommend an excellent analysis of the rise of folklore as linked to an idealisation of the English rural sector in Bennett, G. 'Folklore Studies and the English Rural Myth'. *Rural History.* Cambridge University Press. (1993) 4 1, 77–91.

62 Hutton, R. *Triumph of the Moon: A History of Modern Pagan Witchcraft.* Oxford University Press: Oxford, 1999. 117.

pan-English movement.[63] In my own research in Bungay, for example, as we will see in the next chapter, I found that Bungay was defined predominantly as a centre of regional trade, progress and industry in contrast to the surrounding countryside in East Anglia until the collapse of local industry during the late nineteenth and early twentieth centuries. In this case the issue is not that the English rural myth and romantic approach to folklore were the only (or even dominant) forms of representation of the countryside but rather they became an increasingly popular method which was utilized as a vehicle to form local and national identity and as a response to the perceived negative aspects of industrialism, growing cosmopolitanism and progress.

The construction of rural England as the cultural heart of the nation had several important characteristics. Firstly, it drew boundaries between the popular culture of the city and that of the country by claiming that rural festivals, rituals and folklore were inherently different in character to their urban counterparts. This was drawn primarily through conceptualizing the country as a timeless historicity linked to tradition and integrated with the local rural economy. Rural life was perceived as more authentic and spiritual than urban life. In this light, the only folklore was rural folklore, given that this approach legitimized ritual, belief and mythology primarily through its perceived link to the eternal English identity (or whatever nationality currently under investigation). Secondly, these rituals were significant precisely because they were seen as fossils with which the folklorist could reconstruct the bones, as it were, of authentic culture to find the continuities with which one could formulate a genuine cultural identity. Finally, the underlying aesthetics of this approach constructed the rural sector of English life as a place of magic, wonder and mystery which, in its resistance to industrialism and rational secularism, could offer an escape route from the anxieties and ills wrought by industrialization and urbanization.[64]

The Brothers Grimm provided the vehicle for this approach to folklore in their attempts to define Germanic identity through the collection of the tales and legends of the 'folk' (defined as a separate category through rural locality and perceived isolation from the corrupting impact of industrialization). In their search for an eternal Germanic identity they collated

---

63   Mandler, P. *'Against Englishness: English Culture and the limits to Rural Nostalgia, 1850–1940'.* Transactions of the Royal Historical Society, 6th series 7 (1997). 155–76.

64   Waldron, D. *The Sign of the Witch.* 75.

tales connected to oral traditions and recast them as belonging to time immemorial. For example, in her typography of Black Dog legends Barbara Woods notes that Wilhelm Grimm routinely doctored oral texts in order to have them read like fairy tales. This was most apparent in the shifting of local legends attributed to an individual who lived a decade earlier a short distance away to read as originating 'once upon a time'.[65] In the English context this fairy-tale approach was popularised throughout the nineteenth century but became theoretically fully developed in the work of Tylor and, more significantly in Sir James Frazer's classic text *The Golden Bough*.

The Golden Bough is an enormously significant work. It has achieved iconic status and whilst many of its conclusions and theoretical models have become discredited, or at least heavily criticized, it remains very influential and popular.[66] The text became central as one of the theoretical pillars of the contemporary Pagan revival and a popular approach to British history and nationalism.[67] Even in the case of Bungay's Black Dog we can find repeated references to the claim that it represents an ancient English Pagan survival dating back to the Celts or Vikings.[68] In essence, Frazer argued that there is a teleological development in ritual, belief and culture which evolved from primitive superstition and magic, to organized religion and finally deist enlightenment rationality. If this was the case then a scientific basis for understanding the essence of human social and cultural evolution could be established by studying the world views, beliefs, symbols and folklore of societies left behind after the rise of industrialism and scientific rationality. All folklore, superstition, symbolism and belief in this context represented a window into the past. Folklore could be construed as a science oriented toward discovering truths about human nature rather than an interpretive discipline in the vein of literature or symbolic anthropology.[69]

---

65   Woods, B. A. *The Devil in Dog Form*. 5.

66   Beard, M. 'Frazer. Leach and Virgil: The Popularity (and Unpopularity) of the Golden Bough'. *Comparative Studies in Society and History*. Vol. 34, No. 2 (April 1992) 203-224.

67   Whilst a full study of the influence of 'The Golden Bough' is beyond the scope of this work I would recommend a reading of Beard, M. 'Frazer, Leach and Virgil'. 203-224. Waldron, D. *The Sign of the Witch*. 89–94. Hutton, R. *Triumph of the Moon*. Benet, G. 'Folklore Studies and the English Rural Myth.

68   Eastern Daily Press. Nov. 30. *Eastern Daily Press*. Dec. 8, 1996. *Beccles and Bungay Journal*. Dec. 6, 1996. Westwood, J. 'Friend or Foe: Norfolk Traditions of Shuck'. 74. Stubbs, C. 'A Straunge and Terrible Wunder.' *The Fortean Times*. 30, 32.

69   Waldron, D. *The Sign of the Witch*. 90-93.

Frazer's model with its veneer of scientific credibility, when combined with the idealization of rural England as the cultural basis of the British nation state, had an intoxicating effect on folklorists. The Romanticist panacea of rural life and England's Pagan past, set against the anxieties and social ills of rampant industrialization, social dislocation and urbanization, could now be legitimised with the label of academic credibility. Furthermore, the idealized 'Merry England' could be construed as the authentic basis of English national identity in opposition to cosmopolitan Britain as a modernist empire. This coming together was to have an enormous impact on folklore studies as a whole and formed the basis of numerous cultural revivals and the reclaiming of heritage well into the twentieth century. Its legacy is still apparent today.

Neo-romanticism or the revival of the nostalgic longing for the past as a source of cultural renewal was a central theme of popular culture and a powerful response to the crisis in English national identity during the late 1920s and early 1930s. Movements such as the Ramblers, the Woodcraft Chivalry Association and even early Pagan revivalist movements shared a common culture of anti-modernism and an innate antipathy to industrialism of the Victorian era. These were, nonetheless, oriented to harnessing the symbols of the past, traditional community and the countryside as a vehicle for cultural and economic renewal. When heavy industry and modernization reached its peak in the early twentieth century and then suffered the disillusionment of massive decline and economic hardship during the Depression, the romantic idealized view of the countryside and traditional life rose to stark prominence. Furthermore, this pattern was linked to a broader national invented tradition that linked nationhood with the countryside and English antiquity.[70] The impact of this cultural response to the malaise of declining British power, economy and traditional Victorian era, social life also played a role in redirecting the efforts of the British labour movement from traditional Marxist discourse of class conflict to a romantic idealization of pre-industrial life as an anti-modernist response to the ills of the Depression which played a role in the reshaping of Bungay into a historic town as we shall see in the next chapter.

There were two myth-making machines at work in nineteenth-century England which we argue continue through to the present day. One is defined by the efforts of varying levels of government, the tourist industry

---

70   Trentman, F. 'Civilization and its Discontents: English neo-Romanticism and the Transformation of anti-modernism in Twentieth-Century Western Culture'. Journal of Contemporary History. Vol. 29, No. 4, Oct. 1994. 584, 585.

and academic studies of folklore, seeking to create and define new forms of national identity in response to social turmoil in the rapidly changing face of post-industrial revolution Britain. The other myth occurs at the level of local people who create their own cultural narratives and legends of identity and culture in response to the lived experience of rural life as it evolves in relation to social, demographic and economic developments.

In both cases these myth-making machines work to construct folklore in the established language and cultural forms of English culture. However, far from being static legacies of a primordial past, as they are often represented, these 'myths of antiquity', folklore and superstitions are dynamic responses to contemporary circumstances that draw on images which evoke a feeling of pastness. They are constructed within the established language of cultural, symbolism and shared folklore which both give these representations powerful social meaning and instil them with a sense of authority, community identity and the supposed stability of antiquity. Moreover, this evolving matrix of folklore is developed at different levels of class and locality which, far from occurring in isolation, draw upon each other for legitimacy and meaning. Together they manufacture an infrastructure of myth-creation and interpretation that focuses on a sense of nostalgic antiquity and are a reactionary response to industrialism and the enlightenment and accepted as the basis for legitimating belief and custom.

East Anglia, with its rural economy, the intransigence of its local folk culture and relative isolation from the rest of England was a wellspring for the folkloric approach to culture and antiquity. Similarly, the draining of the Fens in the nineteenth century (after incomplete attempts with the help of Dutch immigrants in the seventeenth century) gave rise to a sense of mystery and lost legacy surrounding the culture of the 'fenman'. Local resistance to the drainage process also drew public attention to a visible image of rural intransigence in the face of modernity through numerous local protests and attempts at sabotage. Together this created an image of a close knit traditional society enmeshed in deeply religious traditions and superstitions, resistant to the changes wrought by science, modernity and industrialism and who maintained beliefs and practices that could be linked to a primordial Pagan past. The long-term colonization by the Dutch also worked to create a unique cultural and linguistic characteristic to Norfolk and forged links with the continent.

Looking at regional examples of Black Dog legends and stories from Norfolk and Suffolk, in *Sixty Years a Fenman*, Randall comments that

Black Shuck or Shucky dogs are an integral part of Norfolk culture. He remembers clearly his parents in the early part of the twentieth century being concerned that Black Dogs would be about on a given night and so would order their son indoors after seeing to the livestock. He would then lock the doors and turn off the lights. The next morning his parents would usually say, 'Well, we'll be hearing of something today,' and he then goes on to claim that the family would be sure to hear of a death in the village. The Dog itself was described as an enormous black, shaggy dog, dragging a rattling chain. He also related a local story of finding a man dead in a home with the pawprints of an enormous hound around the door. The disturbing part of the story for him was that they could find prints lead up to the old man's door but none leading away.[71] In Enid Porter's book, *The Folklore of East Anglia*, she discusses the vast array of Norfolk myths surrounding Black Shuck. She describes multiple stories of a hound with 'Eyes as big as saucers and blaze wi' fire. He is fair as big as a small wee pony, and his coat is all skeffy-like, a shaggy coat across, like an old sheep.'[72] Reeve's book *A Straunge and terrible Wunder: the Story of the Black Dog of Bungay* lists a wide assortment of regional sightings of Black Shuck. Some of the more prominent examples feature a Lowestoft local who saw Black Shuck in conjunction with disaster at sea, a lady in 1929 who saw Black Shuck shortly before a row of cottages burnt down and a Norwich man who recalls cycling home late one night from Norwich where he saw,

The biggest hound sitting by the signpost, that I had ever seen in my life. Its eyes shone like coals of fire. I was sceptical in passing him. But on doing so, he made no move... Half a mile further I heard him, coming up behind, his paws beating the grit road. 'My God he's coming for me'. Instead he passed me so close I could smell his rankness.

The Hound, well in front, suddenly stopped on the fringe of a spinney, in the middle of the road, facing me. To me he looked aggressive... Just then there was a roar of a vehicle, coming through the spinney. It came through with no lights, and was careering from side to side. The great hound was right in its path as he hit it.

The vehicle came so close that I fell into the hedge with my cycle on top of me. The vehicle sped up the lane out of sight. Picking myself up, thinking the hound had come to a bad end, I was amazed to find it still standing

---

71 Randell, A. *Sixty Years a Fenman*. 99–100.

72 Porter, E. *The Folklore of East Anglia*. Batsford Lila: London. 1974. 89–90.

there, as I was sure I saw it struck. I, for the first time in my life, felt fear in my heart, of knowing what the hound would do if he came for me. To my surprise he turned and was gone. Neither left nor right just vanished... On that night he saved my life, for had I been in the spinney I would not be here now. But true to beliefs of country folklore on seeing the dog I lost my dear wife two years after.[73]

These stories historically give both a sense of localization and divergence yet, by the present day, there is clearly a sense of strong commonality between them. Folklorist Theodora Brown wrestled extensively with the problems raised by this vast array of intensely localised myths homogenized together over the course of a century in folkloric discourse. To date, she has conducted the most detailed and in-depth study of Black Dog mythologies. Repeatedly in her notes on Black Dog sightings she asks, 'What are these things?' In a letter to Margaret Murray in response to Murray's repeated insistence of a link between the late medieval witch trials, surviving Paganism and Black Dog myths, Brown stated that 'I cannot imagine any one explanation for our dogs at present.'[74] She put forward the initial distinction between true Black Dogs which only took the shape of a Black Dog and the shape-changing fey creatures that could occasionally take the form of a black hound but just as easily appear in a diverse range of other forms.[75] This insight, whilst making a worthwhile distinction, was also problematic in that the process of categorizing and labelling a wide array of sightings as Black Dogs lay at the heart of the problem rather than anything integral to the phenomena themselves. In this sense, as Jeremy Harte argues, the Black Dog, as a unique English myth and as an icon of the deep countryside is, to a large extent, a creation of folklorists and the organic interaction of researchers, publications, and the people they are studying.[76]

Taking a Jungian-inspired perspective, Brown attempted to eschew a historical study of the origins of Black Dog folklore and examined the archetypal significance of the sightings. Indeed, she argued that on many occasions 'an aetiological myth' had been superimposed on a local piece of folklore surrounding Black Dog sightings to bring the tale in line with the broader literature on Black Dogs. For example, she noticed that the ghost story of Lady Howard in Devon, a hated wealthy landowner of the

---

73   Reeve, C. *A Straunge and Terrible Wunder*. 68.

74   Letter to Margaret Murray in Theo' Brown archives University of Exeter.

75   Brown, T. 'The Black Dog'. *Folklore*. Vol. 69, No. 3, September 1958. 175–192.

76   Hartes, J. 'Black Dog Studies'. 5.

seventeenth century, in which her ghost was believed to have been preceded by a demonic hound with one eye, had been integrated into the broader myth of the Devonshire Black Dog. In this light, Brown's goal was to look for patterns in Black Dog folklore and sightings which gave some insight into the meaning and experience of Black Dogs in English culture and psychology.

From this approach, Brown noted several patterns in people's experiences and in the associated folklore of Black Dogs. Firstly, she found the localized nature of the phenomenon to be extraordinary in that the majority of people through England who had experience of either Black Dog apparitions or folklore to have no idea of the universality and patterning of the phenomenon. She found that most people felt embarrassed or surprised to find that it was such a wide-ranging occurrence. The impact of this provinciality can be seen in the claim by local folklorists in multiple English counties that Arthur Conan Doyle's Hound of the Baskervilles was based on their own local Black Dog having no apparent cognisance of other related tales in other parts of Britain. She also noted that this strong localization of the mythology lent itself against the notion that these stories were simply carbon copied from other parts of Britain despite their apparent similarity. Brown also argued that that Black Dogs are almost all related to a definite locality, such as the Black Dog of Bungay, the Black Shuck of the Norfolk coast and the Black Dog of Newgate.[77]

In trying to make sense of this wide array of stories she proposed that there were essentially three kinds of Black Dog myths. Firstly there are the aforementioned shape-changing fey creatures which sometimes appeared in the form of a Black Dog, distributed over a regional area such as the Black Shuck of the Norfolk coast and Fens or the Barguest of Yorkshire. In local folklore these creatures typically go out of their way to show their supernatural characteristics and can appear in many forms but seem to most often appear as a Black Dog. Secondly, there are also Black Dogs which appear according to a calendrical cycle appearing on a specific date or season. Finally, there are the true Black Dogs which appear as a large black (or sometimes white) dog and assumes no other shape. These Black Dogs are usually associated with a town, family or specific locality.[78] Sometimes this is simply the ghost of a dog associated with local ghost stories but on other occasions, such as the 1577 event in Bungay, the Dog is taken to be a

---

77 Theodora Brown Collection University of Exeter.

78 Brown, T. 'The Black Dog'. 176.

manifestation of the Devil or other supernatural entity.[79]

Perhaps the most important finding in the Black Dog myths and sightings from Brown's work was the extent to which Black Dogs acted as a symbolic parallel of humanity's relationship with dogs in general. This pattern may be seen in related but disparate mythologies around the world dating from antiquity. Dogs associate closely with humans and live closely with them acting as both guardian and protector. Similarly, the heightened senses of a dog, so valued by humanity, are often linked to a belief in a sixth sense and the ability to see into the supernatural realm. Dogs are thought to possess a level of foresight with regard to oncoming danger. Because they are scavengers and predators who aid humanity in the hunt they can also represent a serious threat to life and limb, particularly for the weak and vulnerable members of society.[80] In view of all this Brown argued that perhaps the most profitable way to look at these experiences and myths about Black Dogs is in terms of psychological projections from the unconscious born out of times of great anxiety or danger, such as the turmoil of the Reformation or, of a more immediate nature, the tremendously destructive storm in Bungay on August 4, 1577.[81]

In this Jungian context, the Black Dog can be understood as a projection of the Shadow, the repository of the dark anxieties, desires and drives of the unconscious mind. Because of its primitive and archaic nature, an eruption of the Shadow is unmediated, it emerges autonomous of the conscious and rational functions; it is instinctive and frequently manifested in repressed primal aspects of the self. As such the Shadow and its projection may be apprehended as an object of anxiety, fear and loathing, representing the antithesis of our conscious ideals and sense of self this sense of nameless dread. In this light, the tendency of Dogs to be perceived as linked to boundaries of the spirit world in mythology gives a great deal of resonance to the apparitions of Black Dogs as a manifestation of the dark underbelly of the psyche.

There has long been a close mythological link between dogs and death. Dogs, as carrion eaters and animals usually perceived to have heightened senses, giving access to the other world, are commonly seen as guardians of the gates of life and death in mythology, and are often perceived as

79   Theo' Brown Archives University of Exeter; Westwood, J. 'Friend or Foe: Norfolk Traditions of Black Shuck'. 71–72

80   Theo' Bown Collection University of Exeter.

81   Theo' Brown Collection University of Exeter.

psychopomps guiding departed souls to the next realm.[82] In this context Black Dogs, as a link to the other world, a guide and a harbinger of death, fit very closely within a broader pattern of Black Dogs in mythology that is almost world wide in application, albeit with many regional and local variations. In this sense the association of Black Dogs with deaths works to reaffirm their role as repositories of unconscious anxieties linked with the underbelly of the unconscious.

Another important influence on the development of Black Dog folklore was the claim that the Black Dog mythology could have been linked to medieval witch cults. Margaret Murray, author of *The Witchcult of Western Europe* and one of the founders of the myth of Pagan survivals which underpinned the birth of Wicca,[83] put forward the argument that Black Dog folklore and sightings represented an example of surviving Pagan witch cults. In her correspondence with Brown, and in the minutes of Devonshire Association Folklore Section, she repeatedly inquires as to whether Black Dog folklore and sightings, so prominent in demonological lore surrounding witchcraft in the early-modern period and in the witch trials themselves, were more common in Witch-ridden areas. The implication is that these beliefs in Black Dogs were a legacy of that time and perhaps represented a continuity of these beliefs into the present.[84] However, Brown argued that in her view this was not the case due to the sheer diversity of beliefs and sightings, only a tiny fraction of which are linked to witchcraft and of these, virtually none are linked to witchcraft in the contemporary local imagination. She further argued that Black Dog sightings in English folklore, post-antiquity, were simply not associated with any god or deity nor linked to any known cult activity. She comments that 'It appears when and how it will to the most unlikely of people, sceptics and all, but always in certain situations.' She goes on to add that rather than the appearance of demonic hounds in demonological lore and witch trials being the source

---

82   The role of Dogs as psychopomps and guardians of the other world is extraordinarily common in myth and folklore ranging from classical figures such as Cerebus and Anubis to more obscure figures such as Tezcatlipoca in Aztec belief and is too vast a topic for a full discussion here. For a solid overview of Black Dogs in this mythic role I strongly recommend Stone, A. 'Infernal Watchdogs, Soul Hunters and Corpse Eaters.' In Trubshaw, B. Explore *Phantom Black Dogs*. 16–56.

83   For more detail on the impact of Margaret Murray on the rise of Wicca please see Hutton, R *Triumph of the Moon*. 199-201 and my own analysis in Waldron, D. *Sign of the Witch*. 80–83, 90–100.

84   Theo' Brown Collection University of Exeter. Devonshire Association Folklore Section minutes, hon. Secretary Rev'd W. B. J. Brown para 6.

of the Black Dog myth they, like the Black Dog sightings of the present, are simply both archetypal. In this light, the Black Dog is an archetype deeply entrenched in the human subconscious which medieval Christian discourse absorbed from both the literature of antiquity and in popular folklore.[85] This argument is paralleled by Woods who claimed that the medieval Christian literature of demonic hounds, such as that in Faust, were as much influenced by established popular and oral traditions as they were by religious texts.[86]

In Bungay itself the impact of this folklore during the nineteenth century is very difficult to ascertain. As we will discuss in more detail in the next chapter, Bungay during the nineteenth century, in contrast to much of Norfolk and Suffolk, was a flourishing urban centre. Almost all of the official cultural production and representations of Bungayan identity during the nineteenth century were constructed in terms of local industry, trade and technology. In contrast to the idealization of traditional rural life represented by the Fenman and Suffolk farmer so loved by the Romantics and folklorists, Bungay's mainstream culture, as manifested in print and literature, tended to be that of a progressive centre of civilization, an island in the midst of ignorant superstition and a somewhat backward rural community. While there is a wealth of information on Black Dogs in rural Norfolk and Suffolk, Bungay's written record of local folklore during the nineteenth century is rather ambivalent. Nigel Harvey, in his examination of Norfolk folklore in the 1930s, argued that the Black Dog had not been seen in living memory.[87] Similarly, Woods argued that in her research during the same era, neither the 1577 incident nor the Black Dog of Bungay itself were the subject of local oral tradition or Bungayan folklore.[88] However, these claims contrast with Rider Haggard's depiction of local beliefs surrounding the Black Dog of Bungay during his time in nearby Ditchingham.[89] Brown recorded some tales from the 1920s in and around the Waveney Valley district of a ghostly Black Dog, standing twenty-eight to thirty inches tall, black and shaggy with large glowing red eyes and that

---

85 Devonshire Association Folklore Section minutes hon Secretary Rev'd WBJ Brown para 6.

86 Woods, B. A. *The Devil in Dog Form.* 1. Woods, B. A. 'The Devil in Dog Form.' 229–232.

87 Harvey, N. *Folklore.* Vol. 54, No. 4 (Dec. 1943). 390, 391.

88 Woods, B. A. *The Devil in Dog Form.* 24.

89 Haggard, R. *Farmer's Year.* 26.

would vanish when he came level with you when walking alone at night.[90] Similarly, Hugh Braun, in a letter dated June 28, 1969, wrote to folklorist Brown recalling his memories of Bungay's Black Dog saying,

> I have been familiar with the Black Dog since 1930. I was restoring Bungay Castle in Suffolk and the Black Dog is a local celebrity with a monument over the town cross in the shape of a weathervane. A child of 10 whom I used to escort from school at weekends told me that she knew old Shuck quite well and that he sometimes fell in beside her as she walked to and from school. She had no fear of him and used to be quite sorry when, after a while, he disappeared.[91]

Elizabeth Bonhote, writing in the late eighteenth century whilst living in Bungay, noted that her maid servants were often afraid to walk through St. Mary's churchyard after dark.[92] Similarly, the material found by Brown in her correspondence with locals in Bungay during the 1940s, coupled with a proliferation of Black Dog folklore in the surrounding region, suggests that whilst the Black Dog assumed a far less prominent position in local folklore and civic identity than today, it was far from an unknown local myth.[93] This perspective is further reinforced by the enthusiasm and rapidity by which the local population embraced the mythology of the Black Dog during its revival in the mid-1930s, as we will discuss in the next chapter.

However, this is not to suggest that there is a continuity of belief between the 1577 event and the present. As previously mentioned, the great fire of Bungay in 1688 destroyed much of the town and almost all of the records from that period. The scale of the demographic shift at that time makes a linear oral tradition of cultural continuity unlikely.[94] Furthermore, there were many instances in nineteenth-century literature in which the Black Dog of Bungay tale and related stories of Black Shuck in Norfolk were brought to the fore and entered popular imagination as well as being reinforced by other local myths of Black Shuck in the surrounding district. Perhaps the most pertinent example here is the 1826 reprint of Abraham Fleming's text printed by T & H Rodd in London, a bookseller of some fame due to his collection of rare texts. There was a similar edition with

90   Theo' Brown Collection, University of Exeter; Haggard, R. *Farmer's Year.* 26.

91   Theo' Brown Collection, University of Exeter.

92   Reeve, C. *A Straunge and Terrible Wunder.* 4.

93   Theo' Brown Collection, University of Exeter.

94   Reeve, T. *The Day Bungay Burned.* 27–30.

a woodcut of the Dog charging the aisle of the church accompanied by a poem which has now entered local verse. This is often cited as a local poem despite the author having a very limited grasp of local geography, placing Bungay and Blythburgh in Norfolk near Norwich. This phrase particularly is often taken as a local verse or warning,[95]

> All down the church in midst of fire,
>
> The Hellish monster flew
>
> And passing onwards to the quire
>
> He many people slew.

That being said, the Black Dog of Bungay in recent times is very much a living tradition with its own body of folklore and sightings. The proliferation of Black Dog stories and articles in local media since the 1930s, as discussed in the next chapter, is often followed by a barrage of letters to the editor from readers who have their own tales and experiences of the Black Dog of Bungay. Similarly, discussions with locals brought forth many stories of people's experiences with the Black Dog. Interestingly, as Jennifer Westwood notes, far from the Dog acting as the harbinger of death, its most common role in the more modern tales was as a protector, particularly for young women. A common story was of people seeing the Dog whilst driving late at night as a warning of potential danger on the road or protecting travellers on their way home. Another was of young women in the 1930s and 1940s seeing the Black Dog as a warning not to go out that night as there may be trouble that evening. Perhaps most often I found people simply had seen the Dog and felt emotionally overwhelmed and paralysed by its strangeness. In these later cases the story was not simply one of seeing the Dog act in an overtly supernatural way, but simply that by a sense of strangeness or 'wrongness' about what they had seen. This material seems to parallel that found by Brown, Reeve and Westwood in their own research into the topic. Typically I also found that people seemed embarrassed about their stories. They were felt deeply moved by what they had experienced yet also dismissed it as superstitious nonsense.

This particular experience is commented on extensively by Evans who found that in many of the rural Norfolk and Suffolk people he interviewed

---

95 Reeve, C. *A Straunge and Terrible Wunder.* 63. The original 1826 document and accompanying poem is held in the Ethel Mann Collection: Lowestoft records office.

born in the late nineteenth century and after, there was a contradiction within people who were born into a rich legacy of folklore as an important part of their cultural heritage yet also felt extremely awkward and dismissive of their own beliefs and customs as superstitious and irrational. Evans sees this pattern as the product of people who have been raised with a modern rationalist education yet are brought up in a local culture riven with belief in superstitions, ghost-stories and legends. The juxtaposition of the transformation wrought by new social patterning and fear of ridicule and humiliation regarding local folk culture creates a duality which sat awkwardly regarding peoples' attitudes to local folklore.[96] This pattern still seems evident today with many people I interviewed and spoke with who felt awkward and scoffed at local superstitions but still seemed to feel an enormous emotional connection to these stories rooted deeply in local folklore, culture and superstitions.

This seems to fit very closely with Brown's Jungian model of the Black Dog experience as a projection of the unconscious. Brown was strongly influenced by Jungian analysis. The sheer extent and spread of Black Dog mythologies across such diverse cultures, the enormous emotional power the symbolism has in literature, folklore and belief seem to testify to the archetypal significance of the Black Dog. In this sense the Dog can be interpreted as a psychological projection of the percipient. Nevertheless, Brown also felt that the projection model was inadequate in that it did not explain why Black Dog experiences seemed confined to specific locales in the Bungay area, nor why the sightings were reported by such a diverse range of people engaged in very different activities, people who often displayed no signs of the kinds of psychological stresses linked to powerful projections of the unconscious. Jung however, argued that these kinds of 'hauntings' were projections of 'unconscious autonomous complexes' which, because they have no direct association with the ego or conscious self, seem to act independently of the perceiver. However, this explanation does not adequately account for why people should seem to have these experiences when they do, paralleling each other so closely, occurring in particular locales with particular symbols, as do the Black Dog of Bungay sightings.[97] This dilemma left Brown to leave her book unpublished whilst she searched for an appropriate vehicle to express her findings, examining the impact

96 Evans, G. E. *The Pattern Under the Plough*. 21–25.

97 Main, R. (Ed.). Jung on *Syncronicity and the Parnormal*. London: Routledge. 1997. 55–56

of hypnogogic states, parapsychology and projections, mapped onto actual phenomena.[98]

Another important angle to this psychological perspective is that a significant portion of the folklore surrounding Black Dogs is focused on the importance of narratives surrounding place and heritage as opposed to merely the supernatural issues. In myths and folklore of events like the Black Dog of Bungay there is a powerful undercurrent with regards to local identity, prominent landmarks and the history of that place and its tie to the experience of the people who live there. Ghost stories follow a similar pattern whereby the folklore links people emotionally and culturally to symbols of heritage. These allow people to symbolically grapple with issues of identity, values and connectedness to community and heritage. Ghost stories also retell powerful events from the past, granting the authority of heritage to tales which metaphorically reflect aspects of people's experiences. In the case of the Black Dog of Bungay there is a symbolic connecting of the people of Bungay in the present to powerful formative and traumatic experiences in the Reformation which played a substantial role in shaping the town's present day existence. Similarly, it ties the cultural identity of the town's folk emotively to the Church of St. Mary as the town's cultural and geographic centre. As we will discuss in the next chapter, one of the key local responses to the collapse of local ideals of progress and industry in the early twentieth century was the reclaiming and recentering of town identity on the past as manifested in local folklore, heritage via the medium of folklore. I would argue that folklore has to be looked at holistically, linked to heritage, landscape and local narratives as opposed to trying to study the material as a disconnected supernatural phenomenon.

This brings us to the nature of folklore itself. We began this chapter with the emergence of folklore as a discipline being driven by a sense of loss or the death of tradition. In this sense the authenticity of culture became associated with the idea of the folk as windows into an eternal national identity and reified into the symbol of the nation. Through this process came the notion that folklore was about the search for cultural fossils located in those areas removed from industry and modernism and coupled with a nostalgic yearning for the 'old ways'. Traditions, beliefs and rituals thus became perceived as static gateways to authentic culture. Black Dog

---

98   Theo' Brown Collection, University of Exeter. Harte, J. 'Black Dog Studies' 12–13 and Sherwood, S. 'A Psychological Approach to Apparitions of Black Dogs', in Trubshaw, B. (ed.) *Explore Phantom Black Dogs*. 21–35.

folklore, including the Black Dog of Bungay, became a vehicle to find links to an authentic past, a heritage linked to Vikings, Celts and Saxons. Many of the breaks and incongruities of this material were glossed over under the weight of romanticist aesthetics. However, as we have seen, the folklore of the Black Dog is a living part of a community which has undergone enormous changes over the past centuries and the tale of the Black Dog has evolved accordingly, along with people's experiences. Far from developing in isolation, the language used to describe the mythology, and people's experiences of it, has been profoundly shaped through interaction with other discourses such as folklore and popular culture, despite the parochial nature of such myths. Folklore acts as the informal language of culture through which communities express identity, values and experiences. As such, the Black Dog has become the centre-piece of Bungay's contemporary civic identity and an important link to the town's past. The Black Dog of Bungay inevitably looms large in the town's culture.

4

The Making of 'Old Bungay'

Bungay is a Lady with a 'Past'. A past which is half concealed and half revealed by such evidence as is supplied by her druidic Stone and Fair, both of which originate in that dim and distant pre-Roman period popularly conceived of as Celtic.[99]

The story of the Black Dog, along with the tales surrounding the Bigods, has been a centre-piece of town identity in Bungay for a long time. These stories are also directly linked to the two most prominent historic buildings of Bungay's middle ages, Bigod's Castle on the River Waveney and the Priory Church of St. Mary, home to the 'Straunge and Terrible Wunder' of the Black Dog's attack on the church as chronicled by Abraham Fleming in his tract of 1577. These two icons of local folklore, to be found on the town's Coat of Arms, form the core of the town's folklore and history. In the words of the Rev. Harris, 'Bungay is a Lady with a 'past'.' The town has a strong foundation myth located in the primeval past of pre-Roman Britain and is chronicled by events closely linked to the narratives of English ancestral identity rooted in the rural life of English men and women. Events like the Roman Colonization, the Norman Conquest, the Reformation and the Civil War loom large in the town's construction of historic identity and physical vestiges of that history are clearly visible in the town today and its surrounding district. These stories are also seen in the historic buildings of the town, like the Fleece Hotel and in related narratives, such as the history of the local Grammar School founded in 1565.

Central to this is the sense of historicity and identity, legitimized through links to a distant past found in the landscape, architecture and folklore, creating a sense of continuity moving through tradition, to heritage. Complementing this theme is a strong focus on the history of the

---

99   Harris, H. A. Rev. Foreword. in Mann, E. *Old Bungay*. 7.

aristocracy as remembered through the folklore of the common people. Attempts to make sense of the story of the Black Dog legend have typically focused on either finding a 'true' origin in remote antiquity which further legitimates the myth of a continuous unbroken link to the present, or the use of the tale to legitimate a contemporary supernaturalist perspective. In both cases the tale of the Dog looms large over the folklore and the town becomes a mere footnote to the Dog story. In many ways this does a disservice to the town which gave rise to the myth and provided the social, cultural and historical context in which the tale has evolved, allowing it to become a prominent symbol of town identity, community and solidarity. This chapter will examine the development of the legend of the Black Dog of Bungay in folklore and symbolism as it became the primary representation of Bungay's civic identity during the early- to mid-twentieth century. Further issues to be examined are the major social, cultural and political challenges faced by the local community in the aftermath of the Great Depression and the Second World War. Central to these challenges is the shift in Bungay's local representation from a regional centre of industry and trade to a self-constituted 'historic town'.

As illustrated in Reverend Harris's foreword to Ethel Mann's 'Old Bungay', there is a clear awareness of an attempt to shape the town of Bungay as a self-consciously 'historic town'. This is an important distinction to make. All towns have a history and in Europe and the British Isles many towns and communities have a history of settlement that stretches back into pre-historic times. However, this is different to being a 'historic town', a term which implies both an awareness and consciousness of that history and feeling of historicity as an integral part of local identity. For Bungay, this sense of being shaped by history was inevitable. All around, in landscape and architecture were the symbols of its origins, aided and abetted by the idealism of more than a century of rural romantic story-telling. How could the people of Bungay not feel that this had always been so? The links to the primordial past can be easily observed in the surviving material culture, and in the popular imagination, reinforced by the overwhelming national narratives of Englishness linked to historical continuity. The contemporary attempt to preserve that past and nurture a sense of nostalgia for this past intensifies this process in the popular imagination.

The tale of the 'Black Dog of Bungay', embedded in the imposing presence of the historic and spectacular Priory Church of St. Mary (and more recently linked to the Castle of the Bigods), is very much part of this tradition. The tale and associated myths invokes a sense of mystery and supernatural awe. It brings the folklore of supernatural Black Dogs to the present, together with nuances of Celtic, Saxon, Viking and sometimes even Egyptian mythology. This story takes one of the most picturesque and historical buildings in the town, the Church of St. Mary, and allows it to be situated in the centre of the town's consciousness.

Rooted in local folklore dating back to at least the Reformation, the tales of the Black Dog and the story of the attack in St. Mary's, takes town identity and directly associates it with the rural traditions and customs of the local people. The folklore forms a direct symbolic and spiritual link to the past, creating a romantic narrative of continuity, timelessness and permanence in the face of ever shifting and changing modernity. This identity is also established through the very visible depictions of the Dog symbol. The Black Dog is emblazoned on the town weather-vane. It rides the 1577 lightning bolt that struck the belfry of St. Mary's at the time of the legendary Dog's attack on the people of Bungay. The Black Dog can also be found on the Coat of Arms and numerous other representations in local literature: pamphlets, programmes, games, shop-fronts and titles of local organizations. Bungay boasts the Black Dog Running Club, Black Dog Antiques, Black Dog Football team, Black Dog Marathon and Black Dog Books. In sport, culture, commerce and council, Bungay's identity is tied to the mythical event of 1577.

However, this fixation on historicity as the basis of town identity is far more contemporary than it appears at first glance. Much of the paraphernalia associated with the Dog as the symbol of Bungay's identity dates to the peculiar circumstances which the town faced during the Great Depression and in the aftermath of the Second World War. What appears to be an organic manifestation of local folklore was, in fact, a deliberately constructed attempt to create a sense of historicity. It was an invented tradition utilised to offset the economic and social woes of the Depression. This is not to deny the long history of Black Dog folklore which has been prominent in the local imagination since before the Reformation but to make clear that the appropriation of the hound as a signifier for the township of Bungay is comparatively recent and made as a response to pressing social, economic and political challenges.

Prior to the 1930s Bungay was first and foremost a regional centre of industry and trade. Throughout the eighteenth century the town had the epithet, 'Little London', because of its rapidly growing population and industrial base.[100] Ever since 1672, when an Act of Parliament gave funds for the improving of the River Waveney for trade purposes, Bungay has been a centre of regional trade, manufacture and industry.[101] The old phrase 'Going to Bungay for New Bottoms and New Cuts' was sometimes thought to derive from the periodic need to re-cut and re-bottom the river so as to continue navigation as detailed in S. Ashby's 1826 song.[102] Another interpretation repeated to me by locals is that the phrase related to the thriving Bungay industry in re-bottoming boats. The river trade even from medieval times, and increasingly through the seventeenth to the late nineteenth centuries was a central platform of Bungay's economy. Bungay's position close to the River Waveney had made it an attractive site for settlers in the

The ancient stone in St. Mary's churchyard, thought to have been connected with Druid worship, and also referred to as the "Devil's Stone"

prehistoric era. The river partly encircles the town which, together with its marshy water-meadows, created a strong defensive position. This was further strengthened by earthworks and ditches built during the Saxon period. In the medieval times, the town increasingly prospered from the river trade, for the water-way was navigable to the port of Yarmouth, thus linking it with other important centres for the sale of local produce. In addition it supplied sufficient power for the several water mills on its banks, some of which were in existence from the 1080–86 Domesday

100 East Anglian Magazine. 1975, pp. 58–65.

101 Original document for taxation, bottoming, cuts and trade along the river located in the Ethel Mann Collection: Lowestoft records office.

102 East Anglian Magazine. 1975, pp. 58–65.

Survey. Many of these mills were used for 800 or more years.[103] Like other East Anglian rivers, the Waveney is comparatively slow-moving and had a tendency to silt up from time to time. This had clearly occurred in the seventeenth century, when it became so clogged that it was only navigable as far as Beccles, about eight miles distant. An Act of Parliament passed on Oct. 24, 1670, rendered the river re-navigable by means of four locks at Geldeston, Shipmeadow, Ellingham and Wangford. From that date the trade of Bungay exports greatly increased, particularly in corn, flour, malt and timber.[104] A document, c. 1775, describes the river industry thus: 'The Staithe & Navigation on the River Waveney, navigable for Keels, Lighters, Wherryes, and from the Port of Great Yarmouth in Norfolk to Bungay aforesaid about 30 miles through a fine trading County'.[105]

In 1820, the following lines were penned by a local resident, Samuel Ashby:

> You've heard of Old Bungay – her famed Navigation
> Her Waveney, the pride and delight of the town,
> That brings to her wharf the choice wares of the Nation,
> And adds every year to her wealth and renown.[106]

William Walker and his brother Arthur owned the Staithe Navigation from 1884 and continued the river trade's prosperity. They were well-known millers, maltsters and merchants, who also owned a fleet of wherries some of which were built at the Staithe. The Bungay part of the Waveney was starting to silt up again by the 1920s, and the last owners of the Staithe Navigation were Messrs. Watney, Combe, Reid & Co. who acquired it in 1919.

As well as a boat-building industry and a profitable foundry there were other sources of production linked to regional agriculture. Bungay was also home to a large printing industry and by the end of the eighteenth century there were several printing presses in the township. One of these, established by Charles Brightly and later owned and managed by John Childs, played a national historic role in 1835 when the Oxford Bible monopoly

---

103 Pluck, D. *The River Waveney, Its Navigation and Watermills.* Morrow & Co. Bungay, 1994. 15.

104 Mann, E. *Old Bungay.* 147.

105 Pluck, D. *The River Waveney, Its Navigation and Watermills.* p. 18.

106 Mann, E. *Old Bungay.* 149.

was broken.[107] By law the printing of Bibles was restricted to Oxford and Cambridge Universities and the King's Printer, Eyre and Spottiswoode. John Childs regarded the Bible printing monopoly as a scourge. He ridiculed the excuse that the monopoly was necessary to ensure no mistakes were made in the Holy Book and argued that these printing restrictions prevented affordable copies of the Bible being available to the working classes. His Bungay company was capable of producing low-cost editions of popular books and he could not see why it should not produce Bibles. He fought long and hard gaining the support of men like Lord Brougham who managed to get Parliament to set up a Committee of Inquiry. The eventual result was a breaking of the monopoly and cheaper Bibles.[108] This event was widely celebrated both in Bungay and across the British Isles.

John Childs had become a partner in the firm by 1812 and, following Brightly's death in 1821, he inherited the business which he managed with his brother Robert, and later his son Charles. Through his London printing connections, Childs became acquainted with many of the leading men of the period, including politicians, writers, reformers and Non-Conformists. Under his management the business became one of the best stereotype and printing establishments in the kingdom, employing a large number of local people. In particular his serial publications, the Imperial Edition of Standard Authors, issued in monthly parts, provided high-quality literature at a low cost for an increasingly literate public, and proved an immense success. His son Charles managed the firm following his father's death in 1853. After his death in 1876, the business was acquired by the leading London printers, Messrs. Clay, Son & Taylor. As Clays Ltd, St. Ives plc, it has continued to prosper to this day as one of the world's largest book producers.[109]

Bungay was also a major centre of hemp production. Hemp was farmed throughout the district ranging from Eye to Beccles and Bungay. Since the Enclosure Acts of the mid-eighteenth century it was very rare to find more than five or six acres of hemp in the ownership of one farmer. The sandy loam soil of the region was ideal for hemp and small-scale farming practices tied to seasonal industry, were a back-bone of the local economy until the mid-nineteenth century. Hemp was carefully cultivated and manured directly after planting, providing local employment for seasonal

107   Mann, E. *Old Bungay.* 53.

108   Mann, E. *Old Bungay.* 153.

109   Dictionary of National Biography: John Childs.

Black Dog Antiques shop

Archway over Cork Bricks alley, with ironwork featuring the Black Dog

Black Dog board game, produced in c. 2002

farm labourers. The plants were steeped in local clay pits through a process called 'retting' to separate the fibres and was woven as cloth in local mills. A local speciality was the material known as 'Bungay Canvas' which was used in the sails of fishing boats.[110]

Like much of East Anglia, farming-related industries and associated seasonal labouring were an important part of the local economy. Occupational boundaries in East Anglia were often fluid, with people commonly changing occupations throughout the seasons, depending on the needs of the local economy. Much employment was 'by the job' rather than by trade. In the countryside in particular, trade building and construction work was notoriously short-lived and there was a great deal of movement between one class and another. As Raphael Samuels argues, 'The country craftsman or mechanic was a man with two or three strings to his bow.'[111]

This form of employment, and its centrality in the local economy, has often been neglected by historians due to its fragmented nature. It was difficult to systemically categorize and define in national statistics. Furthermore, the parochial nature of this economic activity meant that much of it failed to show up in national statistics. It was of such a short-lived, or *ad hoc* nature, that it simply failed to register as occupations. In these circumstances the title of farm or field labourer seems to cover all.[112] This pattern of seasonally related work relates closely to the local Cottage economy which consisted of all the unofficial sources of income and resources on which most families relied for sustenance and survival in harder times. Unofficial barter, trade and production was a major part of the economy, along with poaching, which also formed part of the seasonal cycle of work, integrated with the patterns of official industrial production, yet curiously hidden and neglected in local histories.[113]

So while there was a strong drive towards urbanization throughout England during the nineteenth century, the Waveney Valley region, and Bungay in particular, was extraordinarily densely populated. Partly this was due to the rise in population experienced across England during the nineteenth century but also because of changes in the local infrastructure of industry and economy. The demographic explosion of Victorian England

110   Mann, E. *Old Bungay*. 150, Reprinted from the 'Waveney Life Magazine' April 1993, by kind permission of the Editor, Mr V. Mayes.

111   Samuel, R. 'Village Labour'. In Samuel, R (ed.). *Village Life and Labour*. Routledge and Keegan Paul, London, 1975, pp. 4, 5.

112   Samuel, Raphael. *Village Life and Labour*. 1975, p. 3.

113   Samuel, R. *Village Life and Labour*. 1975, p. 6.

was manifested in the countryside as well as the cities and a regional industrial centre like Bungay experienced the brunt of this rapid population growth. It also had an impact on local culture as large numbers of 'itinerants' and immigrants were mobilized into regional industry and agriculture. This had the effect of further breaking up traditional seasonal patterns of labour and fragmented an already rapidly changing community demographic and placed further strain on traditional forms of social organization.[114] In 1822, the Three Tuns Hotel in Bungay was used for the detention of men held in custody for breaking up threshing machines at Woodton, four miles north of Bungay. The workers were protesting against the new farming methods which were causing farm labourers much hardship because their labour was replaced with new machinery. Cavalry had to be summoned from Norwich to disperse the rioters and the ring-leaders were marched off to Norwich Castle and imprisoned pending trial.[115] Nevertheless, a vibrant growing economy and a sense of industrial progress were able to soothe most public concerns about potential damage to tradition, community and identity from industry and economic development.

The sense of Bungay growing into a vibrant centre of local trade and industry seems to be predominant in the literature, media and culture of the nineteenth century. The town song, 'Old Bungay', written in 1826 and sung to the tune of 'Old Roast Beef,' makes extensive references to the town's industry, trade and economic development but none to the town's pre-industrial history.[116] Similarly, in a review of the *Eastern Daily Press* and the *Beccles and Bungay Journal*, along with its forerunner *The Journal*, there was negligible mention of the town's pre-industrial history or economic development until late 1932. When the town's pre-industrial history was brought into focus (such as in the *The Journal*, December 10, 1932, discussion of the 1688 fire which destroyed most of the town) it was not presented as representative of the town's contemporaneous identity but as an analogy to the damage wrought by the 1931 earthquake and linked to the harsh experience of the agricultural, economic and industrial depression of the 1930s.[117]

By all accounts the Great Depression had a traumatic impact on the

114 Samuel, R. Village Life and Labour. 1975, pp. 10, 11.

115 Honeywood, F. Reeve, C. and Reeve, T. The Town Recorder: Five Centuries of Bungay at Play. Peter Morrow & Co: Bungay, 2008.

116 Copy held at Bungay Museum.

117 The Beccles and Bungay Journal, The Eastern Daily Press and The Journal. Accessed through the Lowestoft Records Office.

town of Bungay. In my research I spoke to and interviewed people who had lived in Bungay at the time. They unanimously described the era as one of 'very hard times' and particularly 'hard for farmers and labourers'. The local papers of the early 1930s were solidly focused on the issues raised by unemployment and economic uncertainty. Public uproar from the unemployed and unionised labourers appears to have been a common experience, with the issues commonly presented in quite openly Marxist rhetoric. For example, on July 8, 1933, the *Beccles and Bungay Journal* reports a protest by local unemployed workers and farm labourers who were making the claim that capitalists 'buy from the cheapest market and sell in the dearest market. Business robbery proceeds unchecked.' Furthermore the protest spokesman argued that 'the remedy of poor wages, poor housing and tied cottages is incapable of relieving the suffering of workers'.

In 1933 the River Waveney, accepted as an icon of the town's prosperity, was formally closed for trade. At its peak the river carried extensive produce of malt, coal, corn and flour. It was claimed that local entrepreneur, Mathias Kerrison, had made over a million pounds on the river trade during the Napoleonic Wars.[118] While the river locks had already been out of commission since the mid-1920s, the official closure of the river undoubtedly had a major psychological impact on the already traumatized community. Similarly, Harry Rumsby, proprietor of the local iron foundry, discussed the problems wrought by hard times during the early 1930s in terms of having to take on dozens of 'little fiddling jobs to do outside of our proper work' that he should have refused but was forced to take on in order to keep the small town business afloat.[119]

Another blow was the loss of the Town Pump, already redundant but as a product of local industrial development in 1812, a time of peak economic growth, its destruction in early 1933 by a traction engine owned by Messrs. H. A. Newport was a blow to community pride.[120] Tied up with the longer-term impact of hemp production becoming redundant in the late nineteenth century, the decline in the agricultural economy and the collapse of industries dependent on river trade ravaged the social and cultural fabric of Bungay. These had been the economic foundations upon which the village infrastructure was based. By 1933 the town was described

---

118 East Anglian Magazine. 1975, p. 60.

119 Ewart-Evans, G. *Where Beards Wag All: The Relevance of Oral Tradition.* Faber and Faber, London, 1975. 38, 39.

120 *The Journal.* May 13, 1933.

by the East Suffolk Town and Country Planning Council with these words, 'The town bears an air of industrialism and is dull.'[121]

These issues were endemic across East Anglia and particularly ravaged the seasonally based traditional economy of Suffolk. Ronald Blythe's study of the Suffolk Village of Akenfield discusses the broad sense of economic decline in rural East Anglia from the 1920s through to the full collapse of the Great Depression. One informant describes a pattern of assault on the local village economy beginning with the retracting of the 1917 Corn Laws. These laws, by guaranteeing a stable, subsidized cost for the harvesting of corn, enabled farmers to pay stable wages to labourers who were the back-bone of the East Anglian labour force and regional economy. However, the retraction of the Corn Laws, combined with a harsh hot summer in 1921, resulted in a slump which massively cut into the wages and working conditions of labourers during the 1920s. This decline had a snowballing effect throughout the regional economy which, under the strain of the simultaneous collapse of global trade and industry, disintegrated the local economy in the wake of the Depression. Part of this process was a systematized attack on union membership by farmers and industry which led to an increased sense of class hostility that periodically flared through the region during the late 1920s. This led to further protest and thence to a reduction in both real wages and living conditions. As one of Blythe's informants writes,

> Sixteen men fell out of work but there was no dole for farm labourers. An unemployed farm worker got parish relief but a single man got nothing. So the young men began to walk to other villages searching for odd jobs. Soon East Anglia was full of these men and, by 1930 or so, you'd get up to 50 of them passing the cottage every night as they tramped from workhouse to workhouse.[122]

It was these particular circumstances of industrial decay, social upheaval and class conflict that Dr. Leonard Cane, who was to become the driving force behind the reconfiguration of Bungay as a 'historic town', became Town Reeve. Born in Peterborough in 1882 he was educated at Uppingham King's College in Cambridge and St. Bartholomew's College in London. In 1921 he came to Bungay and partnered in the Trinity Street Medical Practice

---

121 *The Journal*. April 18, 1934.

122 Blythe, R. *Akenfield*. Penguin Books, Harmondsworth, 1969. 47, 48.

with Dr. J. L. Simms.[123] Dr. Cane was described to me by his daughter and contemporaries as a very forthright man who, as an avid amateur historian was fascinated with Bungay's pre-industrial past and worked tirelessly for the recognition of the historical sites, stories and history of the town. After having become Town Reeve in 1932 he began a two-pronged attack on the town's malaise. On the one hand he began with a series of welfare and housing projects designed to alleviate the suffering wrought by the poverty of the Depression. On the other with a civic project for reconstructing the traditions, rituals and architecture of Bungay's past, including the tale and folklore of the Black Dog of Bungay.[124] This latter project was designed to redefine the town's identity and sense of community pride through an antiquity linked to English heritage rather than former industrial wealth.

Before moving onto a discussion of Dr. Cane's project to economically and culturally rejuvenate the town of Bungay, it is worth discussing the peculiar circumstances of his position of Town Reeve which is unique to the town of Bungay. The role of Town Reeve is thought to have developed from Saxon times when the 'tun-gerefa' was elected as the chief magistrate, administering the 'tun' or small township. Other forms of 'gerefa' have survived into modern times, such as Port Reeves, Fen Reeves, and Shire Reeves (sheriffs), but Bungay has uniquely retained the role of Town Reeve as a leading representative of the community.[125] The actual historical connection between the Saxon and contemporary Town Reeves of Bungay remains a matter of debate. In the past, the role in Bungay was more directly involved with public affairs, with the Reeve and his Feoffees elected by the Town Trust, administering many aspects of town life. However, in 1910 the Urban District Council was formed and the elected positions of Chairman and Councillors largely superseded the roles of Feoffees and Town Reeve in local politics. Today, the Reeve heads thirty-four Feoffees, and the role is to administer Charitable Trusts, lands and almshouses for the benefit of the townspeople.

In previous centuries the Town Reeve and Feoffees would have been as unpopular as any group of individuals dealing with townspeople's business. However, once their role was purely charitable they could be perceived in a different light. It was to a great extent Dr. Leonard Cane who, during his

---

123 Personal Communication with Mrs Peggy Clay (Daughter of Dr. Leonard Cane and Margaret English) July 9, 2008.

124 Harris, J. *The Town Reeves of Bungay.* 2nd edition, 1725–2007. Witley Press, Hunstanton, 2007. 45.

125 Harris, J. *The Town Reeves of Bungay.* 9.

first period of office between 1932 to 1934, helped to effect this change. As well as emphasizing and publicizing the unique and historic role of the Town Reeve's office, he appealed to town pride and re-introduced the annual Town Dinner which was open to all who wished to attend and became the highlight of the Bungay social calendar. In addition, he was not a remote figure, as many of his predecessors would have been, but the local family doctor. Many people in the town would have attended his surgeries or received a visit at one time or another and, in that way they, could get to know him on a more personal basis – and even advise him if they thought he was acting unwisely.

During the 1930s, when the economic Depression was casting gloom over the country, other Reeves also decided to introduce popular measures. Hubert Bowerbank, Reeve from 1935-6, created a children's playground on Outney Common, and Guy Sprake, 1936-7, created another one on the Jubilee Road housing estate. Rosalind Messenger, the first female Reeve, 1937–8, acquired the Castle Hills as a public open space for the benefit of the townsfolk and later play equipment was also provided. So it became clear that the Reeves were no longer perceived as the bossy, interfering and self-perpetuating 'clique' that they had been of old, but a new-style group aiming to serve the populace to the best of their ability.

To alleviate the economic and social woes of the Depression, Dr. Cane's first course of action was to develop a series of committees for welfare designed to investigate ways of generating economic growth and alleviating poverty for the people of Bungay.[126] One of the major developments of these committees was the formation of housing trust development bodies and the establishing of allotments to help reduce the poverty of those worst hit by the Depression. This process was aided by engaging in local building projects designed to highlight the town's history and demolishing the decaying remains of nineteenth-century industrialism.[127] This strategy was designed with local economic impact in mind and generated local employment by the use of government and heritage funds which would flow into local businesses and thus instigate economic growth. However, this new economic growth would occur in the context of Bungay as a 'historic town' based on local production and community rather than as a centre for regional trade and

---

126 *Eastern Daily Press*. Feb. 16, 1933. (The external structures of one of the numerous Maltings still stands today near the 'Chicken Roundabout' and is being currently redeveloped as housing.)

127 *Eastern Daily Press*. Feb. 18, 1933.

The Bungay town pump, shortly before it was demolished in 1933.
Courtesy of Bungay Museum

industry. To this effect Dr. Cane also reconstructed traditions long since lapsed, such as the aforementioned Town Dinner (fallen into disuse after 60 years), the Thomas Wingfield Dinner and Sermon (originally established in 1593 to commemorate the founder and benefactor of the Bungay Grammar School). He also began to compile contemporary accounts and scrap-books of local history from print media and other sources. A similar process was enacted for the position of Town Reeve which, under Dr. Cane, became far more ritualized with the creation and revival of invented traditions involving robes, medallions and ceremonies, shifting the position from the image of 'town dictator' as it was described on Dr. Cane's assuming of the role, to the more symbolic role that it plays today.[128]

Probably the most significant of Dr. Cane's historical projects in this respect was the archaeological dig at the ruins of Bungay Castle, located at the centre of town behind the Fleece Inn (itself an historic building dating

---

128   Harris, J. *The Town Reeves of Bungay.* 45; *Eastern Daily Press.* Mar. 3, 1933.

to the sixteenth century). The Castle at the time of Dr. Cane's assuming the title of Town Reeve seemed to be long forgotten under Bungay's history of industrialism and the poverty of the Depression. The Castle itself had been overrun with small-scale cottage industry and shanty construction and much of the Castle had been damaged by Robert Mickleborough's attempts to harvest the stone in 1766. Depictions of the Castle in the mid-eighteenth century showed it to be derelict and dilapidated. By the nineteenth century it was in a perilously ruinous state despite the efforts of Elizabeth Bonhote who had developed a strong attachment to the Castle. Because of her Romantic interest in the castle ruins she had published the novel *Bungay Castle* in 1796 based on her wanderings through the ruins during her time in Bungay. The property had passed in and out of the ownership of the Duke of Norfolk several times and was in a state of extreme neglect. My research and interviews indicated that at the time of Dr. Cane's archaeological dig many people were not even aware that the Castle was there and had little knowledge of its historical significance.

A local woman, Iris Ottaway, recalled that in 1925 she wrote a poem about the Castle which was published in the *Journal*. Several people enquired – 'Well, where is this Castle – we didn't know we had one.'[129] This was hardly surprising as the Castle had become much neglected over the centuries. Even in the fourteenth century it had been described as 'old, ruinous, and worth nothing a year'.[130] Parson James Woodforde visited the site in 1786 and recorded in his celebrated diary that it was 'scarce worth seeing'.[131] Only the lower walls of the original fortress remained, and in the eighteenth century much of its fabric had been hacked away for the sale of road-building rubble. Photographs of the early twentieth century depict it as overgrown with ivy and other foliage and surrounded by an untidy mess of allotment gardens, chicken coops and uncut grass. It is true that in 1920, the King's Head, the town's leading hotel which stands adjacent to the Castle, made mention of the historic ruin in its advertisements, but as the building remained neglected and overgrown very little notice was taken of it as a significant architectural monument with a colourful medieval history. This stands in stark contrast to the fortress from the Norman era where Earl Hugh Bigod could boast that:

---

129   Iris Ottaway, mother of Chris Reeve.
130   Mann, E. *Old Bungay*. 29.
131   Quoted in Reeve, C. *Bungay Castle Guide*, 2001. 1.

If I were I in my Castell of Bungaie, upon the River Wavenie,
I would not set a button by the King of Cockneie.[132]

On July 1, and 8, of 1933, there was a discussion in the *Beccles and Bungay Journal* about the possibility of purchasing the Castle from the Duke of Norfolk as he had expressed no interest in engaging in any archaeological research and restoration and there seemed to be a great deal of anxiety regarding the Castle's future. This was paralleled with a similar anxiety regarding the lack of local employment and the wide-spread poverty associated with unemployment and the collapse of local industry. The sheds, chicken coops and allotments had been cleared by January 22, 1934, and a lease was signed giving the township possession of the Castle on February 26, of that same year.[133] A memorial church service was held in the newly restored castle grounds on April 7.[134] This process of clearing the Castle and ritually drawing attention to it through a church service was closely paralleled by a series of stories and articles on the town's history and the prominent role of the Bigods in the history of East Anglia. Similarly, a story published in the *North China Daily News* of February 11, 1934, on Bungay's historical developments and new direction was reported and discussed extensively in the local media over the same period. This article from a region as far off as Britain's colonies in China was given pride of place in Dr. Cane's personal scrapbook.[135] In this context the redevelopment and embracing of Bungay's heritage represented a renaissance of town identity, prosperity and culture.

The archaeological dig, conducted between November 1934 and July 1935, financed with £460 collected from private individuals and local societies was conducted by Hugh Braun, a well-established architect and later an author on medieval architecture. Living in London at the time of the dig he stayed with the Cane family during the excavations. Of the funds raised for the Castle diggings, approximately two thirds were spent on local labour acting as a source of employment and a boost to local industry. Approximately £200 were spent specifically on the wages of ex-servicemen. The dig also attracted a great deal of local interest and tourism during the summer of 1935 which further added to the funds and local markets.[136]

132 Henry II cited in Mann, E. *Old Bungay*. 31.

133 *Eastern Daily Press*. Jan. 22, 1934, and Feb. 26, 1934.

134 *The Beccles and Bungay Journal*. 1934.

135 *North China Daily News*. Feb. 11, 1934. Bungay's Historical Developments.

136 Braun, H. *Bungay Castle: Historical Notes and Accounts of the Excavation*. Bungay Castle Trust, 1991 (1934). 1, 29.

This was significantly aided by the numerous articles and stories put together by Dr. Cane. He also worked very closely with Hugh Braun and Ethel Mann, whose newly published book *Old Bungay*, worked to bring the town's antiquity to the forefront of the public mind. Hugh Braun and Dr. Cane collaborated in designing official robes for the position of Town Reeve based on medieval artwork and the Town Reeve's civic flag of the Bigod Lion that could be flown from the Castle tower.

It was in this milieu, that the Black Dog became a symbol of town identity. Prior to Dr. Cane's efforts the town was seen as a pathos of economic damage wrought by the Depression. To some extent it was viewed as a scene of post-industrial squalor. By 1935, however, headlines and newsprint stories routinely describe how 'the sun now shines on Bungay' and celebrated the town as a historic monument to English national identity and rural antiquity.[137] The Black Dog mythology first came to the eye of the local media on Saturday April 21, 1933, with a two-page story on the 1577 tale of the Black Dog of Bungay and its links to town history. The article states that 'We hope that the repetition of these stories will serve to create fresh interest in one of the finest churches remaining, not only in this county, but in the whole country.' Throughout the period of Dr. Cane's service as Town Reeve there was regular discussion regarding how the revival of old customs and traditions would lead to the town's renewal and serve as a panacea to the social ills of the economic down-turn of the late 1920s and early 1930s.

The destruction of the Town Pump in 1933 had created a dilemma for Dr. Cane. He wished to establish the site as a place for the town's first electric-light stand. However, the Pump itself, as a product of local industry dating from a time of economic prosperity in 1826, was extremely popular. There was a local outcry regarding its potential demolition and many people argued it should be restored despite its obsolete status as the town had been placed on mains water supply. Dr. Cane's response closely followed his strategy of utilizing the town's antiquity to finance economic, cultural and infrastructure renewal. He decided to follow the story of the Black Dog as 'a memorial to the weather' given that the 1577 event occurred during a 'storm of rain, hail and thunder such as never seen the like'.[138] He put forward the proposal of the weather-vane in the form of the Black Dog of Bungay which gave the new proposed electric standard a close link to the town's antiquity

---

137 *Eastern Daily Press.* Dec. 7, 1934.

138 *Children's Newspaper.* Dec. 23, 1933. *Eastern Daily Press.* Nov. 20, 1933. *Beccles and Bungay Journal.* April 15, 1934.

and tied the Church of St. Mary to the town's heritage and to the extensive work that had been done to restore the Castle.

His strategy was enacted through two main efforts. Firstly, a two-page spread based on Ethel Mann's work 'Old Bungay', including the complete original text by Abraham Fleming combined with the verse from the 1826 reprint was published in the *Eastern Daily Press* along with a historical article on the events and its role in the town's history. This continual reference to the 1577 Dog attack was maintained in local media throughout the period and gelled well with the already established folklore of the Black Dog in the township and surrounding district. Secondly, Dr. Cane's wife, Margaret, organized a competition to be conducted in the local schools for children to put forward designs of the Black Dog to sit atop the electric standard as a weather-vane.[139] The Bungay Council received 150 drawings from Bungay Grammar School, St. Mary's Girl's School, Wingfield Street Primary School, the Roman Catholic St. Edmund's School and All Hallows (based in Ditchingham). These were publically exhibited in the Chaucer Institute during Baby Week of May 1934. The first prize went to Daphne Saunders of the St. Mary's Girls School (Bungay Grammar did not accept female students until 1960) who had submitted three drawings described as 'particularly good'. Second place was awarded to Alec Marshall who attended the Wingfield Street Primary School.[140]

The use of the town's children as the designers for the new standard was a very astute manoeuvre by Dr. Cane as his wife's project drew the local community into the decision to replace the Town Pump by incorporating families into the design process while at the same time disempowering critics who opposed the Town Pump's removal because criticism was now associated with the designs of the children rather than with Dr. Cane. Because the local and even national media showing pictures of Miss Saunders 'proud as punch' of her design becoming a part of the town's history and culture, it would be hard to attack her work personally. My interviews and discussions with Dr. Cane's contemporaries suggested that this was deliberately the case and that he was a very astute individual who knew well how to work the local politics of a small town.

Hugh Braun developed the design for the Black Dog, which is ubiquitous

---

139 Interview with Peggy Clay, daughter of Dr. Leonard Cane, July 7, 2008.

140 Letter from W. M. Lummis to Theodora Brown at the Theo' Brown Collection, University of Exeter. *Norwich Journal*. April 15, 1933. *Daily Mirror*. Nov. 23, 1933. Daphne Saunders with her design.

throughout the town appearing on designs ranging from the local Rotary Club to the Football Club and Town Coat of Arms, into a design suitable for reworking as a weather-vane. Mr H. N. Rumsby built the weather-vane itself. His son recalled the event decades later in relation to the need for work during the early 1930s commenting that,

> About that time we also made the Black Dog at the top of the standard on the traffic island near the market place. Have you seen it? It has a red tongue hanging out of its mouth. It's supposed to be 'Black Shuck' the ghost dog they say used to run around Bungay in the marshes.[141]

Another astute move by Dr. Cane was to associate the new electric standard with the story of the Black Dog. By taking such a prominent piece of local folklore and establishing it as a central part of the town's history, Dr. Cane generated the Black Dog as an integral figure of the town's identity and brought the historic architecture, mythology and narrative of the town together under the one icon. The process of selection also worked to integrate the town into the narrative of Bungay as 'lady with a past' in terms of the shift from a centre of industry to a 'historic town'. Similarly, the continual reinforcement through print media, public rituals and symbols worked to integrate the people, community and culture of the town together under a new identity as a 'historic town' which also became entrenched with the town's emergence from the economic malaise wrought by the Great Depression. In this light the creation of the Black Dog as a centre-piece of town identity, history and culture is a very clear example of what historian Eric Hobsbawm describes as an 'Invented Tradition'.

Invented traditions, according to Hobsbawm, are networks of practices, rituals and symbols designed to promote and inculcate values, ideals and identities through repetition which creates a sense of continuity with the past. Furthermore, by ritually and symbolically using images, stories and folklore that are already connected with the past, this process evokes nostalgia and a powerful emotive feeling of pastness which reinforces the values and ideals connected with the revived tradition. In a sense these invented traditions are contemporary responses to a novel situation which take their reference from popular representations of the past as a metaphor of the present.[142] In the case of the invented and revived historical traditions of Bungay by Dr. Cane

---

141 Ewart-Evans, G. *Where Beards Wag All: The Relevance of Oral Tradition.* Faber and Faber, London, 1975. 38-39.

142 Hobsbawm, E & Ranger, T. *The Invention of Tradition.* 1, 2.

these were a response to the collapse of the traditional economic and social order of nineteenth-century East Anglia through an attempt to reconnect with symbols, icons and ideals located in contemporary representations of the past. For Bungay, it was very much a sense of looking to the past with an eye to the future. Dr. Cane's strategy consistently utilized the town's history as a vehicle for its economic, cultural and social restructure into a 'historic town' from the older sense of town identity as a regional centre of Victorian trade and industry. Similarly, as one respondent commented, by focusing on the issues of the ruling classes in the past, the antagonism of the working classes of the 1930s could be circumvented and restructured in the context of tradition and history rather than class conflict.

Well-established custom, along with the folklore, culture and working life of East Anglia, acted as the infrastructure through which this pattern of invention of tradition could operate. As Hobsbawm and Ranger argue, custom is the motor and the fly-wheel within which tradition can be invented.[143] Dr. Cane was able to make drastic changes to the town's architecture, economy and culture but only in the context of established custom and tradition. Hence the replacing of the Town Pump with the Black Dog standard and weather-vane had to occur within the context of the town's community life, tradition and sense of history if it was to be accepted as

Dr. Leonard Cane, (centre) who organised the excavations at Bungay Castle in 1933. Courtesy of Bungay Museum

143   Hobsbawm, E. & Ranger, T. *The Invention of Tradition*. pp. 2, 3.

legitimate. Dr. Cane did just that. By linking the modernization of the town's infrastructure with community through the competition, folklore with the image of the Black Dog and tradition with the tale of the Black Dog's attack on St. Mary's, he made a controversial decision to modernize the town and transformed it to a statement of tradition, heritage and continuity rather than looking to its past economic glories.

Perhaps the most central reason why Hobsbawm's model is so appropriate here is that the reconfiguration of Bungay as a 'historic town' from a town with a history is that the transformation of 1930s Britain, is one of the central focuses of Hobsbawm's research. It relates to the deliberate and systemic construction of tradition within the rules of custom by the nation state and regional government to promote the sense of nationalism tied to heritage, culture and identity in a distinctly national context. Historic towns in this sense become icons of the English traditional way of life that provide the cultural basis, folklore and heritage of the nation as opposed to empire and industrialization as the centre of British identity. In this sense rural East Anglia ceased to be perceived as a back-water impediment to British industrialism as it was in the late eighteenth and early nineteenth centuries but becomes an icon of eternal Englishness and the cultural basis of the English people.

Despite its origins slipping to the background of public knowledge of the history of the Black Dog, Miss Daphne Saunders's iconic image was solidly established as the symbol of the town by the late 1940s. During the 1930s the coach of the Bungay football team had taken upon himself the title of Lord Bigod and his successor in 1948 called himself the Black Dog. The football club in turn took on the image as the symbol for the Bungay football team and the title of 'The Black Dogs' shortly thereafter. In a letter sent to Theodora Brown by the then Anglican Vicar of St. Mary's, the Rev. W. M. Lummis in 1948, a current pamphlet of the football team featuring the iconic symbol of the Black Dog upon a bolt of lightning was enclosed indicating that the symbol as an iconic representation of the town was already firmly established. In fact in a later letter to Theodora Brown in 1948 he remarked on jokes at his first service there on August 4, 1946 (the anniversary of the 1577 event), that his own recently passed away black dog might run up the aisle replaying the original event.[144] In the 1951 Festival of Britain pamphlet, the Black Dog was also displayed as a symbol of the town's identity a year before it was taken up as a symbol of the town's Coat

---

144   Theo' Brown Collection, University of Exeter.

An early photo of the iron foundry, c. 1900, where the Black Dog
weathervane was produced. Courtesy of Bungay Museum

of Arms. Similarly, the Black Dog appeared prominently above the Butter
Cross in the banner of the Bungay Rotary Club established in 1951.

The town Coat of Arms itself was designed in 1950 by Mr Hellis
Tomlinson who, in terms of the traditional motif for a Coat of Arms,
designed the icon with the Red Lion of the Bigod family prominently
displayed rising from the Castle.[145] This was the design put forward to
tie in with the coronation of Queen Elizabeth II in which the context of
attempting to tie the local English heritage with the pomp and pageantry
of the English monarchy would have had the most impact. However, the
Town Council rejected this image and put forward their own design which
replaced Bigod's Lion with the icon of the Black Dog designed by Daphne
Saunders in 1934. Dr. Cane described the Coat of Arms in an official guide
to the town as 'a pictorial representation of Bungay Castle, standing above
the River Waveney, above the gateways is the shield of Hugh Bigod, the
Norman builder of the Castle in 1164.[146] There floats on the river a wherry,
as a reminder of the water-borne trade that used to be carried upstream as
far as Bungay. The crest is the Black Dog of Bungay courant proper upon a

145   *Beccles and Bungay Journal*. Sept. 22, 1950.

146   Cane, L. B. Dr. *Bungay Suffolk. The Official Guide to the Town and District.* 1954.

flash of lightning. The Rev. W. M. Lummis in a letter to Theodora Brown commented that 'When Bungay was granted a Coat of Arms the Black Dog appeared as the Crest. The designer and I both wished it to appear in chief.'[147] The Town Reeve at the time, Mr John Marshall Clay who married the Daughter of Dr. Cane, Helen Margaret Cane, was also the chairman of the football club. It was suggested to me that the prominence of the Black Dog as a symbol of the football club would have integrated well with its

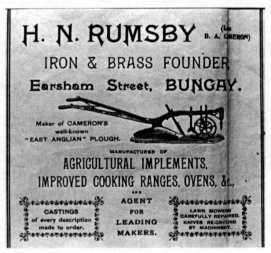

H. N. Rumsby: advertisement for the iron foundry where the Black Dog weathervane was made in 1933. Courtesy of Bungay Museum

prominence on the town Coat of Arms, replacing Bigod's Lion. Mr. Clay, as the Town Reeve would have been central to discussions along with Dr. Cane and the Rev. W. M. Lummis as to the design and it is extremely likely he would have played a prominent role in its selection. The suggestion at the time was that the Black Dog was already by that stage seen as the quintessential representation of the town identity, far more than Bigod's Lion. Furthermore, by selecting the Dog along with Bungay Castle and the River Waveney, the Coat of Arms symbolically tied together the three most prominent aspects of the town's past. The Coat of Arms application cost the town approximately 100 pounds financed by public depositions collected by the Town Council.

The motto itself is very indicative of the invented traditions approach taken with the reconstruction of Bungay as a 'historic town': 'Moribus Antiquis Pareamus' (Let Us Hold Fast To The Old Virtues). My research

---

147   Theodora Brown Collection, University of Exeter.

The Black Dog weathervane in Bungay Market Place, shortly after it was erected in 1933.

indicated that at the time there was some discussion and controversy over both the Coat of Arms design and the motto. One question was 'Why keep to the 'Old Virtues?" [148] This was responded to in terms of the centrality of Bungay's history and culture being an integral part of town identity and the motto and Coat of Arms were symbolic links, connecting the past to the present. Similarly, there was some inquiry as to why the traditional Lion of the Bigods was replaced with the contemporary image of the Black Dog. Dr. Cane responded by iterating that the focus was not on the crest but the Shield of the Bigods and that the Black Dog was a unique facet of Bungay's heritage and folklore.

Since the 1930s the Black Dog has become both the official symbol of civic identity and a symbolic representation of popular town identity. Outside of the issues raised by tourism and pop-cultural representations which will be discussed in the next chapter, the image and story have developed certain sacrality as a symbol of the town. For example, when the weather-vane was taken down for repairs in 2002 it provoked an enormous outcry among local townsfolk and in the local press, this outcry becoming particularly prominent when the repairs took longer than expected. The

148   *Beccles and Bungay Journal.* Oct. 1953.

Black Dog weather-vane and standard was more than a product of local industry, it had come to represent the spirit of the town as it were and its removal was an assault on both civic and cultural identity. Similarly, the Rev. Stephen Morgan, author of a novel based on the 1577 story and former Anglican Vicar of Holy Trinity and the Priory Church of St. Mary, Bungay, wrote a letter arguing against a proposed statue of the Black Dog to commemorate the 2000 millennium being constructed in St. Mary's churchyard in the centre of town. In the letter he argued that as in the 1577 pamphlet the hound was described as a manifestation of the Devil it was not really an appropriate statue for the sacred ground of a churchyard.[149] The letter provoked a flurry of responses for and against the statue, divided between those who agreed with Stephen Morgan's position and those who defended the statue as a manifestation of town identity that transcended its religious origins.[150] Another claim was that the Dog was of pre-Christian origin and therefore beyond Christian concerns of it being a manifestation of the Devil.[151] Stephen Morgan in discussion claimed to have been rather surprised by the level of response and commented that he had written a very general letter drawing attention to the described origins of the Dog story in Fleming's original pamphlet and asking people to 'Just think about it, a statue of the 'devil in such a likeness' in a church? Is that really the best idea?'

Stephen Morgan's own novel is written as a medieval detective story in the vein of the 'Cadfael' books with a large dose of irony and satire. In the book he combines both events of the 1577 incident with tongue in cheek references to people and places of Bungay today and uses footnotes and pseudo-historical research to make fun of the 'invented traditions' nature of many of the town's claims to antiquity, such as the claim that the 'Chicken Roundabout' (the roundabout, at the village of Ditchingham by the Maltings, populated by a group of wild chickens and looked after by a local volunteer caretaker) is in reality descended from the chickens brought by the Saxon invaders of the sixth century. The book itself implies a sense of ironic awareness of the nature of invented traditions and their prominence in town identity in both a mythic and a symbolic sense, defining town

---

149 *Beccles and Bungay Journal.* Nov. 29, 1996.

150 *Eastern Daily Press.* Nov. 30. *Eastern Daily Press.* Dec. 8, 1996. *Beccles and Bungay Journal.* Dec. 6, 1996.

151 *Eastern Daily Press.* Nov. 30. *Eastern Daily Press.* Dec. 8, 1996. *Beccles and Bungay Journal.* Dec. 6, 1996. Westwood, J. *Friend or Foe: Norfolk Traditions of Shuck.* 74.

identity and promoting a connection to the past. Stephen Morgan ties this story to the broader national narratives of folkloric identity, borrowing the tale of the Tower of London Ravens, claiming that according to folklore if the Chickens should ever leave the roundabout at Ditchingham death and destruction will befall the town of Bungay.[152]

This pattern of evolution has continued to this day with the rise of many stories surrounding the Black Dog taking root since the 1950s with some being taken up by the townsfolk and becoming an integral part of the folklore while others are laid by the wayside or perceived with comical amusement. The central theme driving this process is closely linked to the centrality of antiquity and invented tradition in the Black Dog mythology. Claims which tie the central landmarks, characters and buildings of the town are developed, absorbed and promoted with great enthusiasm while others which feel disconnected from the model of Bungay as a 'historic town' and its associated customs are quickly dismissed. There is a discourse around the nature of the Dog mythology, its role in shaping town identity and the narrative of the history of the town that was firmly established on the basis of the invented traditions developed by Dr. Cane and others and shaped by the custom and folklore of the community. This structure, firmly rooted in neo-Romanticism and a nationalist sense of local history tied to local identity has become the foundation upon which the legitimacy of myths surrounding the Black Dog in the local community is founded.

The claim put forward by Anthony Hippisley Coxe in his 1973 book *Haunted Britain*, for example, that the Black Dog is 'the transmogrified soul of Lord Bigod' has been taken up with great enthusiasm by the Bungay population despite there being no prior record of this claim prior to the early 1970s.[153] This story, which was taken up by the *Eastern Daily Press* in the same year and quickly became a feature of public perception of the Black Dog linked to the second of the two most prominent buildings in the town and a central figure in the town's history and foundation myth. This story has been taken up and presented numerous times in the local media, school classes, and the town history as presented in a dramatized version during the Bungay Summer Festival. The Black Dog itself remains a popular subject at the local schools with students regularly selecting the tale as the basis of artwork, fiction, play and games. Similarly, the claim that Arthur Conan Doyle based his novel *The Hound of the Baskervilles*

---

152   Morgan, I. S. *The Kettle Chronicles*. Diggory Press, Liskeard, 2006. 16.

153   Coxe, A. *Haunted Britain*. Hutchinson: London, 1973. 105.

on the Black Dog mythology of Bungay has been taken up very strongly with mentions to this effect in the local media. This parallels the claim put forward by Peter Haining in *The Supernatural Coast* that the novel was developed during Doyle's stay at Cromer Hall and was based on the story of the Norfolk Shuck, a claim that was also displayed at the Norwich Museum.[154] In contrast the claim put forward by Janet and Colin Bord[155] that the Black Dog may be linked to ley lines and UFOs was met with a lot of amusement with one person making the following comment,

> It makes perfect sense; the Aliens are heading back to Alpha Centauri or somewhere and want to stop at the Fleece for a pint. They let the Dog out to go to the toilet and next thing you know he's run in the Church across the road.

In this context there is a clear pattern by which the town's population are aware of representations of their Dog tale in the global environment but are very selective as to what myths can be accepted and incorporated into the broader folklore and which are to be ignored as either an outsider point of view or alien to their community identity. This is well evidenced by the view among the townspeople today that the Black Dog of Bungay is not the same mythic creature as the Black Shuck of Norfolk in contrast to nineteenth- and early twentieth-century claims to the contrary. There are antecedents to this differentiation of Black Shuck as a mythic trickster creature of the Norfolk coast from the demonic Dog of St. Mary's turned symbol of town identity. For example, in her field notes, Theodora Brown argued that the Black Dog of Bungay is a true Black Dog which appears exclusively in the form of a hound in contrast to the trickster shape shifting Black Shuck of Norfolk.[156] However, the insistence of this division which does not seem to have been as prominent in the 1930s, works strongly to differentiate Bungay as a community from the broader East Anglian region and reaffirms the Dog's role as an exclusively Bungayan symbol.

There is a very evident desire to tie the story which has become so central to the town's identity to a narrative that presents local history in the broader context of a locally based English nationalism. This pattern is

---

154 Haining, P. *The Supernatural Coast: Unexplained Mysteries of East Anglia*. Robert Hale: London, 1992. Westwood, J. 'Friend or Foe: Norfolk Traditions of Shuck'. 74.

155 Bord, J & C. *Alien Animals: A Worldwide Investigation*. Granada Publishing, London, 1980. 103, 104.

156 Theo' Brown Collection, University of Exeter.

intrinsically linked to a sense of connectedness to local place and identity, often manifested in the search for themes that contextualized local myth in Pagan antiquity. It is a theme which ties together the landscape, people, architecture, folklore and culture into a coherent whole which creates a sense of connectedness, historicity and authenticity. These themes, developed by Dr. Cane in his use of invented and reconstructed traditions to restructure the former industry centre into a 'historic town', have become firmly entrenched as the centre of town identity and culture. The Black Dog is now unequivocally the central feature of Bungay's civic, cultural and folkloric identity and is firmly integrated into the cultural identity of the community. Today the Dog has shifted remarkably from its perceived Demonic origins into a largely positive symbol of town identity and continues to evolve along with the experiences, culture and society of the people of Bungay and will continue to do so for a long time to come.

The Bungay coat-of-arms, featuring the Black Dog crest.

Conclusion

The Popular Legacy of the Black Dog

Flames licked around the sacred spire

And the congregation's last line of defence was engulfed in fire

And as the flaming priest stepped into the firing line

On the business end of despair

God he took his own life

During the coming of the

Black Shuck, Black Shuck

– The Darkness – Black Shuck

So runs a verse of the lyrics to 'Black Shuck' as played by the Glam Rock band 'The Darkness' in their album *Permission to Land*. The band, originating out of Lowestoft on the coast only a few miles away from Bungay, describes the events of 1577, albeit with considerable dramatic artistic license. The band 'The Darkness' is itself a group which takes an ironic over-the-top approach to retro 1980s rock music of the kind made famous by the mockumentary *This is Spinal Tap*. Growing up in Lowestoft they would have been very much aware of the local folklore and integrated the song with the high fantasy styling and riffs of 80s rock. It is an example of the flexibility of local folklore when integrated with global popular culture where the story becomes told through the media, music, images and language people are familiar with. For that matter, Black Dogs and Hell hounds have featured prominently in popular music of the twentieth century since the 1920s with Robert Johnson's *Hellhound on my Tail* as an example of a very influential early variant.

Representations of Black Dogs which bear strong echoes of the Black Dog of Bungay story are very common in popular culture. A simple search of the internet will bring forth dozens of glossy dramatic representations of the Bungay and Blythburgh tale; YouTube contains dozens of visual representations and there are hundreds of websites dedicated to the story. There are also many references to Black Dogs and the Black Dog of Bungay in books on the supernatural, hauntings, paranormal activities and cryptozoology. Role-playing games such as 'Dungeons and Dragons' and 'Vampire the Masquerade' feature variants on Hell hounds, Barghests and Shucky Dogs, some of which specifically feature variants on the Black Dog of Bungay. Many computer games feature a Black Dog as an antagonist. The award winning and extremely popular computer game *The Witcher* features a major subplot involving a small rural town haunted by a Black Dog called The Beast which has been summoned by the hidden sins of the community to wreak havoc. Black Shuck is also a major antagonist in the online computer game *Lusternia* as well as *Final Fantasy IX*. Black Dogs feature prominently in the television series *Supernatural* linked to Robert Johnson's song *Hellhound on my Tail* and the myth of selling one's soul to the Devil at the cross roads. Black Dogs appear in the Harry Potter series as the Grimm in *Prizoner of Azkaban; the Runton Werewolf* features a Black Dog along with dozens of other fantasy novels.

More recently the Black Dog of Bungay has become the focus of crypto-zoologists intrigued by the notion that they may have both existed in flesh and blood form[157] and been some previously undiscovered form of animal in the manner of the urban folklore surrounding wild big cats such as the Australian 'Gippsland Panther'. For example, Francis Di in her book 'Cat Country', speculates that the creatures described as Black Dogs are in actuality the same as those described as ABCs (Alien Big Cats) linked to sightings and occasional film and photographs of large black cats taken across the British Isles (indeed around the world much like Black Dogs). She argues that many eye-witnesses describe the Black Dog as having a curious lope, more characteristic of a big cat than a dog. On a few occasions eye-witnesses described Black Dogs as vanishing into, or up, trees and ripping open rabbit hutches and the like and she argues many of the paw

---

157 It is also interesting to note that Clare Painting-Stubbs's masters thesis into the history of the Black Dog of Bungay was originally inspired by her discovery on an archaeological expedition of a large canine tooth dating from the Iron Age approximately 1700 years ago. In her preface she comments that her interest in Black Dogs in folklore and history emerged out of her initial zoological curiosity in the extinct wildlife of Britain. Stubbs, C. *Religion, Familiars and Abraham Fleming*. 2

prints looked more like that of an enormous cat rather than that of a dog.[158] This view was also suggested in Chris Reeve's report of an elderly Bungay resident who claimed the Black Dog was in reality the Devil in the form of an enormous Black Cat and recalled a song from her childhood which ran,

Scratch Cat of Bungay

Hanging on the door,

Take a stick and knock it down,

And it won't come anymore.[159]

The mythology of Black Dogs has left an undeniably strong and lasting legacy in contemporary popular culture since the nineteenth century. Furthermore, these representations of Black Dogs in popular culture, whilst originating out of local folklore surrounding Black Dogs across both Britain and the world, have also worked to shape local interpretations of the mythology. In this respect there is a curious process of mutual transformation at work whereby academic, popular and local interpretations of the legend work to interconnect, shape and influence each other. At the same time, in an increasingly cosmopolitan and interconnected world, it is very difficult to clearly ascertain the origins of various representations of the Black Dog let alone clearly define the boundaries between these interpretations. Rather, stories like that of the attack on St. Mary's Church in Bungay become part of a broader melange of Black Dog tales that integrate together in popular culture globally and in turn affect local representations of that mythology.

Perhaps the prime example of this is the antecedent of the Sherlock Holmes novel *The Hound of the Baskervilles* by Arthur Conan Doyle. The story has an enormous legacy and influence and is often considered as the quintessential Sherlock Holmes tale. The tale of the haunted legacy in rural England and the haunting of the moors by an enormous spectral hound is one which immediately calls to mind similar tales such as the one in Bungay. The *Bungay Society Newsletter*, for example, during the 1980s contains numerous references to *The Hound of the Baskervilles* being at least strongly influenced by the Black Dog of Bungay legend and related

158 Frances, D. Cat Country: *The Quest for the British Big Cat*. David & Charles inc: Vermont. 1983. 116–137.

159 Reeve, C. *A Straunge and Terrible Wunder*. 71.

stories of Black Shuck throughout Norfolk.[160] The claim is perhaps most clearly argued by Peter Haining in his book *The Supernatural Coast* where he claims many aspects of the Sherlock Holmes novel were derived from Conan Doyle's stay in Cromer, Norfolk. Haining's argument is essentially that while on a shared holiday with Fletcher Robinson at Cromer, chance led to Doyle becoming aware of the local stories of Black Shuck and these served as the catalyst for the novel and a profitable sharing of Black Dog stories. This claim has entered regional wisdom as the basis for the famous Holmesian story.[161] Similarly, Rider Haggard who was very much aware of the story of the Black Dog of Bungay, was a colleague and friend of Conan Doyle and it is argued that there could also have been a strong influence on the story from that quarter. Norfolk origins are not mentioned in Doyle's preface to the story where he claims the story originated from Fletcher's recounting of Black Dog legends in Dartmoor where the novel is situated. Dartmoor has its own Black Dog mythology, much like that of Norfolk and the story of the Baskervilles closely parallels the remarkably gothic legend of Squire Richard Cabel, a rather malevolent local historic figure from the era of the English Civil War. However, whilst it is unlikely that *The Hound of the Baskervilles* was specifically based on Black Shuck, let alone the Black Dog of Bungay, these regional tales formed a central part of the Black Dog mythology which Doyle would have drawn upon to write his novel. Conversely, from the 1970s onwards the local figure of Hugh Bigod has been increasingly depicted in a manner resembling that of the squire in the Holmesian novel and Squire Richard Cabel's tale, beginning with Hippsley Coxe's claim that the Black Dog of Bungay is none other than the 'transmogrified soul of Lord Bigod' in 1973.[162] Similarly, much like the 1998 film *The Black Dog*, starring Patrick Swayze, I have heard many people both in Bungay and even as far afield as Australia, describe a sighting of the Black Dog late at night on the road as a sign that they needed to pull over and rest before driving as they were likely to have an accident.

Another important legacy of Black Dog folklore is its use as a euphemism of depression. Folklore and mythology resound with legends and myths of Black Dogs, werewolves, hellhounds and the like, associated with death, suffering and the spirit world and from this has emerged the idea of the

---

160 From the West Stow Annals and Bungay Society Newsletters held at the Lowestoft records office.

161 Westwood, J. 'Friend or Foe? Norfolk Traditions of Shuck'. 74.

162 Please see Chapter 4 for more details.

Black Dog as a symbol of depression and misery. Similarly, the long folkloric association of the Black Dog and the Devil works to reinforce the representations of Black Dogs as the cause of misery. Phrases like 'having the Black Dog at your heels' or 'on your back' are routinely used to describe people's emotional suffering. Perhaps the most iconic use of the Black Dog imagery in this way is Winston Churchill's infamous Black Dog. Similarly, as we have already mentioned, the Australian 'Black Dog Institute of Depression' uses the story of the Black Dog and specifically the Black Dog of Bungay as part of their own interpretation of the history of associating Black Dogs with depression and despair.[163] Indeed as early at the seventeenth century the Black Dog was already being used as a term synonymous with a state of melancholia.[164]

The development of Black Dog stories, mythology and folklore is indicative of the process by which popular culture, academic and folkloric studies of the Black Dog mythology intersect and work to shape each other in an organic process of development. It is not so much a case that people consciously take fiction and apply it to folklore, though this does occur. Rather, popular culture is part of the language by which people express meaning, identity and values as part of the process of story telling. As we have discussed through this book, the story of the Black Dog of Bungay is closely linked to the experiences, culture and community of the people of Bungay and they cannot clearly be separated. Hippsley Coxe's claim that the Black Dog of Bungay is the cursed soul of Lord Bigod becomes part of the language used to tell the story because it resonates with the people who tell the story and ties together a wealth of features and expressions of meaning found in the story. It is not simply a matter of historical validity in empirical terms or of a series of events, easily separated into fact and fiction. It is myth-making, tied to the experiences and shared community of the people of the town. In this context, the legend is a product of popular culture, academic studies of folklore and history, and local legends and tales from other regions integrated as part of the cultural milieu. In the cases where a person has uncanny and strange experiences, such as are illustrated by the many sightings of the Black Dog of Bungay, they reach, as we all do, to their framework of cultural reference to make sense of it and try to

163 Hanley, S. The Black Dog Mystery. www.blackdoginstitute.org.au/media/eventscal/indexcfm 5–6.

164 Radden, J. The Nature of Melancholy: From Aristotle to Kristeva. Oxford University Press. Oxford, 2000. 12.

communicate it in the language and shared symbolism of their community.

Mikel Koven in *Film, Folklore and Popular Culture* argues that many folklorists have been very concerned about the extent to which popular culture, particularly that of television and cinema, has worked to homogenize divergent local cultures into a single global consumerist culture.[165] However, whilst the motifs and images used to communicate ideas is certainly shaped and extensively influenced by the impact of popular culture, it is far from being supplanted and reconstructed by this process. There are powerful underlying narratives and ideas at work in local folklore, such as historicity, the role it plays in community cohesion and identity, and its symbolic function in the community. So whilst the image of the dog, or its role, may change over time as we have seen so far in this book, there are structures that govern its development which are profoundly related to issues faced by the community that has created it and maintained it as an integral part of their culture. What has happened is that the symbolic language by which people describe the story has grown and developed along with the cultural changes globalization has brought, all exacerbated through the pressures wrought by challenges facing the community, such as the economic decline of the Depression.

In this way local stories become associated with related images and ideas from the global milieu of popular culture in which they live. There is a complicated but organic development of local folklore as communities become more integrated into a global culture. That being said, this global consumer culture is far from the homogenous consumerist culture engulfing local identity as is often portrayed. As we have seen in the town of Bungay during the later half of the twentieth century, people incorporate these global ideas into the context of their own experiences and the living communities in which they function. So whilst the story has changed and developed with the advent of popular culture, it is still very much interpreted in the context of the living community of Bungay.

The legend of the Black Dog of Bungay is also the story of the town, its people and history. The development of the story over time, and the way it has changed over the centuries, is directly and intrinsically linked to the experiences, trials and tribulations of the community. The sites of the story are the central architectural and geographical features of the town and serve as symbols of the town's history and identity. The origins of the

---

165 Koven, M. *Film, Folklore and Urban Legends.* Scarecrow Press Inc: Plymouth. 2008. 5.

legend in the 1577 event chronicled by Abraham Fleming are born out of the horrendous social strain and conflict of the Reformation. The tale is part of the demonological folklore which gave rise to the witch trials of East Anglia during the social upheavals of the Civil War. The Black Dog's rise to prominence in British Folklore is linked to the massive upheavals of the industrial revolution, and its adoption as the symbol of Bungay's civic identity emerged out of despair at the Depression and the collapse of the local economy. The story of the Black Dog of Bungay is also the story of the town and its people which are both unique and thoroughly entwined with the Black Dog in folklore around the world.

References

Beard, M. 'Frazer. Leach and Virgil: The Popularity (and Unpopularity) of the Golden Bough'. *Comparative Studies in Society and History*. Vol. 34, No. 2 (Apr 1992).

Bennett, G. 'Folklore Studies and the English Rural Myth'. *Rural History*. Cambridge University Press. 4. 1. (1993).

Blythe, R. *Akenfield*. Penguin Books, Harmondsworth, 1969.

Bord, J & C. *Alien Animals: A Worldwide Investigation*. Granada Publishing, London, 1980.

Braun, H. *Bungay Castle: Historical Notes and Accounts of the Excavation*. Bungay Castle Trust, 1991 (1934).

Brown, T. 'The Black Dog'. *Folklore*. Vol. 69, No. 3, September 1958.

Brunvand, J. H. *The Study of American Folklore: An Introduction*. 4th Ed. Warton: New York, 1998.

Burchell, S. *Phantom Black Dogs in Pre-Hispanic Mexico*. Heart of Albion Press: Loughborough, 2007.

Burris,E. 'The Place of the Dog in Superstition as Revealed in Latin Literature'. *Classical Philology*. Vol. 30, No. 1. Jan 1935.

Cane, L. B. Dr. Bungay Suffolk. The Official Guide to the Town and District. 1954.

Chambers, R. *The Book of Days*. Vol. 2, Philedelphia: J. B. Lippencott & co. 1869.

Collinson, P. *The Birthpangs of Protestant England*. Macmillan: London, 1988.

Coxe, A. *Haunted Britain*. Hutchinson: London, 1973.

Crouzet, E. *Slender Thread: The Origins and History of the Benedictine Mission in Bungay 1657-2007*. Downside Abbey Books: Bath, 2007.

Dale-Green, P. *Dog*. Hart-Davis: London, 1966.

Dasent, J. R. (ed.) *Acts of the Privy Council of England, Vol. X, A.D. 1577-1578*. London: HMSO, 1895.

Dutt, W. A. *Highways & Byways in East Anglia.* MacMillan: London, 1901.

Ewen, C. L'Estrange (ed.) *Witch Hunting and Witchtrials: Indictments for Witchcraft from the records of 1373 Assisez held for the Home Circuit A.A. 1559-1736.* Kegan Paul, Trench Trubner & Co: Broadway House, 1929.

Ewart-Evans, G. *The Pattern Under the Plough: Aspects of the Folklife of East Anglia.* Faber and Faber. 1966.

Ewart-Evans, G. *Where Beards Wag All: The Relevance of Oral Tradition.* Faber and Faber, London, 1975.

Forby, R. *The Vocabulary of East Anglia.* Vol. II, J.B Nichols and Son: London. 1830 (1970).

Frances, Di. *Cat Country: The Quest for the British Big Cat.* David & Charles inc: Vermont, 1983.

Grace,F. 'The Battle of Bungay', 1514–1518, *Suffolk Review,* Vol. 5, No.1, Summer, 1980.

Groome, W. 'Suffolk Leechcraft'. *Transactions of the Folklore Society.* Vol. 6, No. 11, June 1895.

Haggard, R. *Farmer's Year: Being the Common Lore Book for 1898.* Longman Green & Co: New York, 1899.

Haining, P. *The Supernatural Coast: Unexplained Mysteries of East Anglia.* 1992.

Harris, J. *The Town Reeves of Bungay. 2nd edition, 1725–2007.* Roseland Publishing, Morrow & Co. Bungay, 2007.

Harvey, N. *Folklore.* Vol. 54, No. 4. (Dec. 1943).

Hobsbawm E. and Ranger, T. *The Invention of Tradition.* Cambridge University Press; Cambridge, 1983.

Honeywood, F. Reeve, C. and Reeve, T. *The Town Recorder: Five Centuries of Bungay at Play.* Peter Morrow & Co: Bungay, 2008.

Hutton, R. *Witches, Druids and King Arthur.* Hambledon Continuum: New York, 2003.

Hutton, R. *Triumph of the Moon: A History of Modern Pagan Witchcraft.* Oxford University Press: Oxford, 1999.

Koven, M. *Film, Folklore and Urban Legends.* Scarecrow Press Inc: Plymouth, 2008.

Lummis, W.M. *The Churches of Bungay*. British Publishing Company Ltd: Gloucester, 1950.

MacCulloch, D. *Suffolk and the Tudors: Politics and Religion in an English County*. Prentice Hall: London, 1986.

Main, R. (ed.) Jung, C. G. *Jung on Syncronicity and the Parnormal*. Routledge: London, 1997.

Mandler, P. 'Against Englishness: English Culture and the limits to Rural Nostalgia, 1850-1940'. *Transactions of the Royal Historical Society* 6th series 7 (1997).

Mann, E. *Old Bungay*. Heath Cranton Ltd: London, 1934.

Morgan, I. S. *The Kettle Chronicles*. Diggory Press: Liskeard, 2006.

Newman, L. F. 'Some Notes on the Folklore of Cambridgeshire and the Eastern Counties'. *Folklore*. Vol. 56, No 3. Sept. 1945.

O'Giollain, D. *Locating Irish Folklore: Tradition, Modernity, Identity*. Cork University Press: Cork, 2000.

Ojade, J. O. 'Nigerian Cultural Attitudes to the Dog.' *Signifying Animals: Human Meaning in the Natural World*. Routledge: New York, 1990.

Page, W. Victoria County History of Suffolk. Vol. 2, 1907.

Painting-Stubbs, C. *Religion, Familiars and Abraham Fleming: An Attempt to Explain the Strange and Terrible Wonder of 1577*. Submitted 21st September 2001 in fulfilment of a Masters Degree at the University of Kent.

Pluck, D. *The River Waveney, Its Navigation and Watermills*. Morrow & Co. Bungay, 1994.

Porter, E. *The Folklore of East* Anglia. Batsford Lila: London, 1974.

Samuel, R. (ed.). *Village Life and Labour*. Routledge and Keegan Paul: London, 1975.

Randell, A. *Sixty Years a Fenman*. Routledge and Keegan Paul: London, 1953.

Reeve, C. *A Straunge and Terrible Wunder: The Story of the Black Dog of* Bungay. Peter Morrow and Co: Bungay, 1988.

Reeve, T. *The Day Bungay Burned: The Story of the Great Fire of Bungay 1688*. Peter Morrow & Co: Bungay, 1988.

Robinson, R. *God's People in Bungay and Denton: The Story of Bungay's Independent*

Church, Later to be Called the Congregational Church (United Reformed & Methodist), 2009.

Trentman, F. 'Civilization and its Discontents: English neo-Romanticism and the Transformation of anti-modernism in Twentieth-Century Western Culture'. Journal of Contemporary History. Vol. 29. No. 4. Oct. 1994, pp. 584, 585.

Trubshaw, B. (ed.) *Explore Phantom Black Dogs*. Heart of Albion Press: Loughborough, 2005.

Waldron, D. *The Sign of the Witch: Modernity and the Pagan Revival*. Carolina Academic Press: Durham, 2008.

Wilby, E. *Cunning Folk and Familiar Spirits: Shamanic Traditions in Early Modern British Witchcraft and Magic*. Sussex Academic Press: Brighton, 2005.

Woods, B. A. *The Devil in Dog Form: A Partial Type Index of Devil Legends*. University of California Press: Los Angeles, 1957.

Woods, B. A. 'The Devil in Dog Form.' *Western Folklore*. Vol. 13, No. 4, October 1954. 229-235.

Archives

Ethel Mann Collection: Lowestoft Records Office

Theodora Brown Collection: University of Exeter.

Newspapers

The East Anglian Magazine

Eastern Daily Press

Beccles and Bungay Journal

The Journal

North China Daily News

Bungay Children's Newspaper

The Daily Mirror

Appendix A:

A Straunge and Terrible Wunder

The following is taken from British Library Printed Book C27 A4, *A Straunge and Terrible Wunder* by Reverend Abraham Fleming. All original spelling, syntax and grammar remains, although abbreviated words have been written in full.

A strange
and terrible Wunder wrought
very late in the parish Church
of Bongay, a town of no great distance from the citie of Norwich, name-
ly the fourth of this August, in the yeere of
our Lord 1577, in a great tempest of violent raine, lightening, and thunder, the
like whereof hath been sel-
dom seene.
With the appearance of an horrible shaped thing, sensibly perceived of the
people then and there
assembled.
Drawen into plain method according to the written copye.
by Abraham Fleming.

...God warneth us by signs from
heaven, by fierie apparaunces
in the aire moste terrible, by
wonders, wrought on earthe,

Strauge & unusiall, by exinun-
dations of waters beyond their
appointed limits, by the remo-
ving of senselesse trees from the
naturall place where they were
planted, by the great power
which the Prince of darknesse
through Gods permission and
sufferaunce hath recovered by
many late moste misserable
murthers not be named, much
lesse to be committed among
Christians, by insurrections
full of daunger and detestable
treason on this side the seas, by
tumults and uprores between
Princes of forreigne nations,
and what should I say more? By
the trump of his sweet and hea-
venly Gospell, sounded unto us
out of the mouths of his messen-
gers. But wee will not be warned, wee will tumble still upon
the bedde of wantonesse, and
drink ourselves drunck with
the wine of sensualitie, that
while wee lye wallowing in the
sinck of our Sodomitical sinne wee
may bee consumed with a
Sodomiticall or a Babylonicall destruction

God open the eyes of our hartes, that wee may see in what
Wildernesse, among what
wilde Beastes and devouring
Serpentes wee doo wander: and
give us mindes mollified and
made soft, that at his woorkes
we may feare and bee astonish-
ed

The occasion that I have
wrote this warning (which I
would to God I had the grace
to follow) was a wonder lately wrought in Norfolke, and
So lately wrought, that the ter-
rour of the same is this instant freshe in memorie. A
spectacle no doubt of Gods
judgement, which as the fire of
our iniquities hath kindled, so
by none other meanes then by
the teares of repentance it may
bee quenched. The order of
the thing as I received the same
I have committed to paper, for
the present viewe and perusing
of those that are disposed. It
is grounded uppon trueth, and
therefore not only worthie the

writing and publishing but
also the hearing and
considering

The reporte of a Straunge
and wonderful Spectacle
Sunday being the four-
rth of this August in
the year of our Lord 1577.
to the amasing and sin-
gular astonishment of
the present beholders
and absent hearers at a certain towne
called Bongay, not past tenne miles
distant from the citie of Norwich,
there fell from heaven an exceeding
great and terrible tempest sodein
violent between nine of the clock in the
morning and tenne of the day aforesaid
this tempest took beginning with a
rain, which fel with a wonderful force
and with no lesse violence then abundance, which made the storme so much
the more extreme and terrible

This tempest was not simply of raine
but also of lightening and thunder the
flashing of the one whereof was so rare
and vehement and the roaring noise
of the other so forceable and violent

that it made not onely people perplexed in minde and at their wits end
but ministered such straunge and unac-
customed cause of fear to be conceived
that dumb creatures with the horror of
that which fortuned, were exceedingly
disquieted and senselesse things void of
all life and feeling shook and trembled

There were assembled at the same
season, to hear divine service and common prayer, according to order, in the
parish Church of the said towne of Bongay, the people thereabouts inhabiting,
who were witnesses of the straunge-
ness the rarenesse and sodenesse of the
storm, consisting of raine violently fall-
ing, fearful dashes of lightening, and terrible cracks of thunder, which came with
such unwonted force and power, that
to the perceiving of the people, at the
time and in the place above named
assembled, the Church did as it were
quake and stagger, which struck into
the harts of those that were present
such a sore and sodain feare that they
were in a manner robbed of their right
wits

Immediately hereover there appeared

in a moste horrible similitude and likenesse to the congregation then there present
a dog as they might discerne
it, of a black colour: at the sight whereof,
togither with the fearful flashes of fire
which then were seene moved such
admiration in the minds of the assemb-
blie that they thought doomes day was
already come.

This black dog, or the divel in such a
likenesse (God hee knoweth al who worketh all) runing all along the body of the Church with great swiftnesse,
and incredible haste, among the people,
in a visible fourm and shape, passed between two persons, as they were kneeling uppon their knees, and occupied in
prayer as it seemed, wrung the necks
of them bothe at one instant clene back-
wards in somuch that even at a moment
where they kneeled they straungely dyed.

This is a wonderful example of Gods
wrath, no dout to terifie us, that we
might feare him for his justice, or pul-
ing back our footsteps from the pathes
of sinne, to love him for his mercy.

To our matter again. There was at

the same time another wonder wrought:
for the same black dog, stil continuing
and remaining in one and the self same
shape, passing by an other man of the
congregation in the Church, gave him
such a gripe on the back, that therewith
all he was presently drawen togither
and shrunk up, as it were a peece of le-
ther scorched in a hot fire: or as the mouth of a purse or bag, drawen togither
with a string. The man, albeit hee
was in so straunge a taking, dyed not,
but as it is thought is yet alive: whiche
thing is mervelous in the eyes of men,
and offereth muche matter of amasing
the mind

Morover, and beside, the Clark
of the said Church beeing occupied in
cleaning the gutter of the Church
with a violent clap of thunder was
smitten down, and beside his fall had
no further harme: unto whom beeing
all amased this straunge shape, whereof
we have before spoken, appeared, howbeit he escaped without daunger: which
might paradventure seem to sound a-
gainst trueth, and to be a thing incredible: but, let us leave thus or thus to
fudge, and cry out with the Prophet

O Domine! O Lord, how wonderful art thou in thy works!
At the time that these things in this order happened, the Rector, or Curate of
the Church, being partaker of the peoples perplexitie, seeing what was seen,
and done, comforted the people, and exhorted them to prayer, whole counsell
in such extreme distresse they folowed,
and prayed to God as they were assem-
led togither

Now for the verifying of this report
(which to some wil seem absurd, although
the sensiblenesse of the thing it self con-
firmeth it to be a trueth) as testimonies
and witnesses of the force which rested
in this strange shaped thing there are
remaining in the stones of the Church
and likewise in the Church dore which
are mervelously rented and tone, the marks
as it were of his clawes or talans. Beside that all the wires, the wheeles, and
other things belonging to the Clock,
were wrung in sunder and broken in peces.

And (which I should have tolde you
in the begining of this report, if I had
regarded the observing of order) at the
time that this tempest lasted, and while

these stormes endured, the whole church was
so darkened Yea with such a palpable darknesse, that one persone could not
perceive another, neither yet might dis-
cern any light at all, though it were les-
er then the least, but onely when the great
flashing of fire and lightening appeared.

These things are not lightly with violence to be over passed, but precisely and
throughly to be considered

On the selfsame day, in like maner,
into the parish church of anothe town
called Blibery not above seven miles distant from Bongay above said, the like
thing entred, in the same shape and similitude, where placing him self uppon
a maine balke or beam, whereon sometime the Rood did stand, sodainely he gave
a swinge downe through the Church, and
there also, as before, slew two men and
a lad, and burned the hand of another
person that was there among the rest of
the company, of who divers were blasted.

This mischief thus wrought he flew
with wonderful force to not little feare of
the assembly, out of the church in a hi-

deous and hellish likenes.

These things are reported to be true yea
by the mouthes of them that were
eye witnesses of the same, and therefore
dare with so much the more boldnesse
verifie what soever is reported

Let us pray unto GOD, as it is the
dutie of Christians, to work all things
to the best; to turne our flintie harts into
fleshie hartes, that we may feele the
fire of Gods mercy, and flee
from the scourge of his
justice...

* *

*

Imprinted at London by
Frauncis Godly dwel-
ling at the west end of
Paules

Appendix B:

Verses Included in the 1826 reprint of the 'Straunge and Terrible Wunder' Pamphlet by Abraham Fleming published by T & H Rood.

Of wondrous things we often read
And hear from time to time
And without doubt they are decreed
By Providence Divine
To awaken sinful mortals to
Repent and understand
Their sins will prove their overthrow
And Judgement is at hand.

The Scriptures plainly testify
That in the latter days
Great signs and wonders in the skye
On earth and on the seas
Of wars and dreadful famines which
Shall scourge the earth below
And plagues and pestilences such
As man did never know.

A wonder strange and terrible
As man did ever hear
Both singular and horrible
Occurr'd in Norfolkshire
At Bungay and Blighborough
Upon the Sabbath day

The people went as custom was
Unto the church to pray.

But in the midst of morning prayer
To everyone's surprise
Darkness did overspread the air
And quite concealed the skies
And rain and hail came rattling down
With such a dreadful roar
The oldest person in the town
Ne'er witness'd such before.

The winds did blow a fearful blast
Which made the church to quake
And sheets of lightning thick and fast
The walls and doors did shake.
And long and loud the thunder roll'd
Tremendous was the sound
Its terror struck on every soul
Some fainted to the ground.

The Church appear'd a mass of flame
And while the storm did rage
A black and fearful monster came
All eyes he did engage.
All down the church in midst of fire
The hellish monster flew
And passing onwards to the quire
He many people slew.

Many were stricken to the ground
Whereof they strangely died
And many others there were found
Wounded on every side.
The church itself was rent and torn
The clock in pieces broke
Two men who in the belfry sat
Were killed upon the spot.

This wonder strange and terrible
Is left upon record
To show to ages yet unborn
The terror of the Lord.
Fearful and wond'rous are his ways
Who can withstand his might?
The great JEHOVAH let us praise
Him let us serve aright.

Appendix C:

Poems from Pupils at Bungay Primary School, from a 2004 display of student artwork in St. Mary's Church

The black Dog is fearce he stops and kills people when he sees them. The black Dog is black one stormy night he raced into the church and killed peaple. He bit and crunched into there bodys like he was eating a biscuit. There was blood all down the iles.

(original spelling and punctuation retained)

All on a summer's day

When people were in church

The sky turned black and stormy

And rain poured down with hail.

A black beast flew through the window . . .

Glass shattered everywhere

His eyes stared fiery-red.

Screaming children hid

Adults stayed silent and still

Until the devil ran -

Growling, howling, grabbing,

Suffocating.

In seconds he vanished

Leaving behind the dead bodies.

Lightning Source UK Ltd.
Milton Keynes UK
06 May 2010
153846UK00001B/34/P